AUPALUKTUK – THE RED ONE

On 10th June 1955, the Canadian Government's Department of Northern Affairs and National Resources wrote to the Hudson's Bay Company advising that the name LUNAN LAKE (latitude 64 degrees 52 North and 93 degrees 05 West) had been approved. This was, they continued, named for Mr. Sandy Lunan of Baker Lake fame and they noted that, although the present policy was to wait at least until individuals had retired before perpetuating their names, when the name LUNAN was put forward, it was considered an exceptional case.

This is his story.

To Graeme and to my oldest friend Barbara
without whose nagging and continual excouragement
this book would never have been finished.

ABOUT THE AUTHOR

 Brenda Ogilvie and her husband Graeme have two grown up sons, Duncan and Andrew. For most of their married life Graeme and Brenda have lived abroad, in Africa, the Indian sub-continent and Greece. During this time Brenda wrote a number of stories, some of which were broadcasted on the BBC World Service.

She spends time in Bournemouth and Southern Spain where she lives.

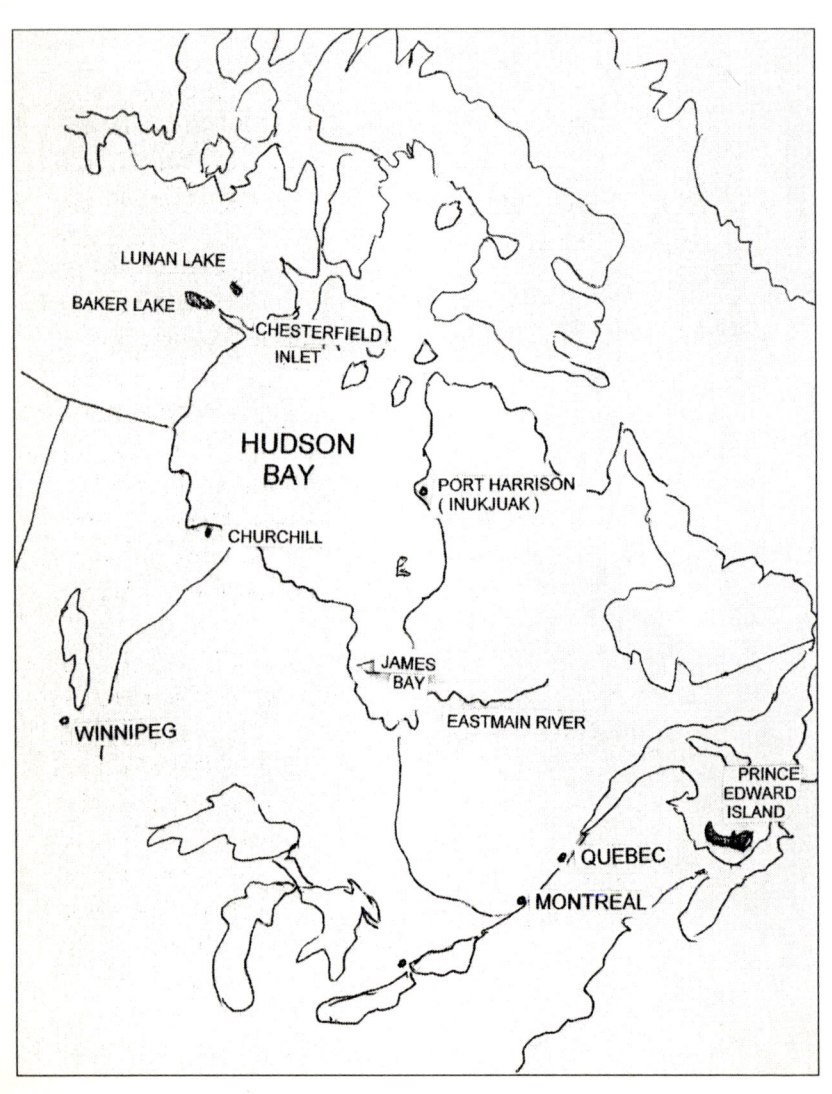

PROLOGUE

Akumalik smiled at the two people sitting opposite her. The woman had her head down and her hand was poised over a pad of writing paper. The man was embarrassed. He wanted to talk to her but could not find the right questions to ask. He would never find the right questions because what he thought he wanted to know was unimportant. He was speaking again and the girl interpreter sitting beside Akumalik turned to her to translate.

She barely listened although she widened her smile and nodded in a pantomime of attention. Her mouth was almost toothless but her smile was sweet, like that of a baby. She had understood before Lucy had attempted to turn his meaningless questions into Inuktitut. He wanted her to tell him about the Red One and yet he asked about the house: how many rooms did it have; had the Red One, who they called Sandy, kept a dog; had he grown vegetables?

She had enjoyed it at first. They had brought her to the big back room in the store, given her pastries and tea and introduced her to the man and his wife, big people with anxious faces, eager to please her and gain her confidence. The man had explained, through Lucy, that the Red One had been his uncle, that he had come to Baker Lake to research and document his life, that she, Akumalik, who had been his housekeeper for so many years, could help them. They had brought photographs, beautiful big glossy pictures, and she had laughed in wonder as she saw herself again, a handsome striking woman in her thirties, taken over fifty years ago. But as they turned the pages of the album there was the face of the Red One, and her heart had grown painful and she no longer wished to remember.

She answered their questions and watched as the woman's hand flew along the page, recording her every word. But she knew it was all pointless.

It was too late, she was too old, they were from a different world and a different age. If all they wanted from her were facts then she had done her duty. But she suspected they had hoped for more and she knew now she could not share her memories with them. Even if they had asked the right questions.

They thanked her profusely. They were good people, she liked them and wished them well in their task. She wondered if the book they had mentioned would ever be written. What did it matter anyway? She would not read it. She would be dead probably and with her would die, in spite of their efforts, the essence of the Red One. The one they called Sandy Lunan.

CHAPTER 1

He first heard of the Company from one of the lads in the army. The Hudson's Bay Company. It practically ran Canada, his informant told him – trading, fur trapping – and they were always on the lookout for men like Sandy. "Hard weather men," they called them; "fit to withstand the rigours of a long Canadian winter," demanded the recruiting notices. Well, he had lived through twenty Scottish winters and come to no harm. *I probably am the right material*, he thought, with all the arrogance of youth and no comprehension whatsoever.

But the time was not right. He was fighting the war to end all wars and he was in Kenya. He listened with interest and then stored away the information in a corner of his mind to be mulled over and reviewed at a later date, when this carnage was over, when escape from the family had again become paramount.

Sandy remembered the recruiting posters – "Your country needs YOU" – with the dramatic bearded face of Lord Kitchener, his finger seeming to point directly at Sandy, who, with thousands of others, had shown up at the depots. But his reasons had been different. One of only three sons in a family of ten, he bore the heavy burden of their expectations. As the youngest of the boys, he was suffocated by the attentions of his sisters, who loved him to distraction, bossing and bullying him affectionately from morning till night. The Kitchener poster had not so much plucked his patriotic heartstrings as shown him the path to freedom.

He knew he owed his family everything. He was clever, had shown early promise. Sacrifices had been made on his behalf to ensure a good education, a fee-paying school, the uniform he needed and the outings he wanted. His father was only a tenant farmer but somehow he managed to find the necessary money and Sandy was always the one who benefited. His guilt at causing unhappiness was matched only by his knowledge that if he did not escape their eternal expectations of his gratitude and the fulfilment of their hopes, he would end up resenting and perhaps even hating this family of his.

It had been a stunning blow when he was initially rejected. Oh, they wanted him all right. He was young, intelligent, fit – officer material. But...

"Anderson-Grice is an essential trade, you are an apprentice engineer there. Recruitment deferred," he was told by the recruiting officer. "Try again next year, that's if it lasts that long." It was a cruel disappointment, made even keener by his sisters' obvious delight. It seemed the longest year of his short life.

But at last he was accepted, when so many young men were needed to replace the ever-increasing casualties of the trenches. The 5th regiment of the Black Watch welcomed Alexander Lunan and trained him as a signals officer. He waited with fascinated dread for the order to move to France or Belgium. But Britain also had to protect her Empire and Sandy found himself seconded to Kenya, fighting a distant but important war against the maddening sting of the German army led by their brilliant commander and strategist, Colonel Lettow-Vorbeck. It was little different from the European war, thought Sandy in brief periods of reflection; two paces forward and then two paces back, maintaining the status quo. An absolute victory never seemed to be a possibility or even an objective, yet the preservation of the East African territories for Britain was essential, keeping her pride and her Empire intact.

On a personal level, Sandy was content. While others sobbed quietly into their pillows at night, racked by the pain of homesickness, he understood and sympathised but revelled in his new life, the discipline, the physical demands made upon him but most of all the maleness of it all. He toughened quickly, and learned even more quickly. He met the bullies and the sadists but found he could deal with them. Isolate or humiliate them and they soon turned to easier targets. He was a leader of men, whose soldiers respected him, admired him, listened to him. He was fair, open-minded, above all he was consistent and they knew where they stood with him.

Privately, he questioned the military decisions of the Generals. From Europe they heard of the impossible numbers of dead, of the shell-shocked, destroyed young bodies and minds, senselessly sacrificed because of stupidity or pride. But these thoughts he kept to himself.

And then it was all over. The Armistice was signed and the world apparently came to its senses again, licking its wounds and hopefully learning from its mistakes. Captain Alexander Lunan was free to go home.

He toyed with the idea of re-enlisting. It was a good life in the Army and he had proved that he fitted in. They were eager to keep him. But he had too many doubts. His sense of fair play was constantly tested by the arrogance of superior officers, superior only in rank because of an accident of birth, gentlemen in name alone. The old boys' club was his stumbling block. He had accepted them in wartime because it was demanded of him, it was his duty. Now he had a choice, he could stomach them no longer.

He wondered then about staying on in Kenya. It was a land full of opportunity. Fortunes could be made in coffee-growing, farming, mining. Sandy had grown up on a farm, he had trained as an engineer, possessed skills that would serve him well in this beautiful country. But again, the doubts reared their heads. He hated the attitude of the white man towards the black man, the unquestioning sense of superiority. Even amongst the most enlightened, where there was kindness and benevolence, it was as a father to a child – but a child who would never grow up and be given responsibility or pride or independence. So many times he wanted to protest but, guilty in his silence yet sensing the futility of a one-man stand against the injustice, he chose to leave.

Scotland it would have to be. Ahead lay his duty to his family, to the sisters who wrote daily of their eagerness to see him again and of their plans for him. He left sadly, the over-powering attentions of those who loved him creeping towards him like a thick, suffocating fog.

But there was a light, a possibility. The Company.

CHAPTER 2

It felt strange to be back in the small Scottish town where very little seemed to have changed during his long years of absence. Men had been away to the war, to France and Belgium, but since this was a farming and fishing community, they were few. Most had stayed working the fields, bringing in the food which was as essential to the war effort as the fighting had been. And even those who had crossed the Channel found Sandy's stories of Africa too foreign, too remote to be understood or acceptable. In the end he stopped telling.

They took Sandy back at Anderson-Grice. He had been a first-class apprentice, now he was a man of many talents; as an ex-captain of the Black Watch, he had overseas experience. To his surprise, he settled well at first. The family, grateful and excited that he had returned safely to them, were slightly in awe of him. He had left them five years ago, their youngest son, but now they saw a man easy with himself, self-confident and used to bearing authority. The sisters attempted to take their familiar place as his advisors and manipulators but quietly and without fuss, he went his own way. His place high on the pecking order was established and in the beginning that was enough.

He renewed his friendship with his great boyhood chum Dom Demarco and together the young men would haunt the dance floors, eye up the young ladies on the promenade, play a round of golf. It was only with Dom that Sandy was able to share his memories and experiences of the war. Dom had lived a very different type of war. The son of an Italian family who had emigrated to Scotland and made a good living in the ice-cream business, he had been unprepared for the prejudice and hate that had been directed at them by the majority of the good citizens of Carnoustie. Eyed with suspicion and distrust, "Wop-spy" hissed at their retreating backs, their business faltered and almost failed. But they were interrogated and not arrested, watched but not imprisoned, and if the authorities were satisfied, then, reasoned the townsfolk, the Demarcos could be given the benefit of the doubt. Besides, their ice-cream was the best on the East coast, its reputation had even reached the English and, where there were tourists attracted by the golf and the beaches, money would roll into the coffers of the shop-keepers and the councillors of the town.

Sandy was horrified by Dom's stories. He in turn could tell his friend of the hatred and injustice meted out to the blacks by the white minority in Kenya. With all the fervour of youth they railed against prejudice, oppression and the suppression of freedom. They discussed with sadness the apparent futility of the war they had both, in their own ways, fought. But mostly they enjoyed themselves.

They were an attractive pair: Dom, tall, romantic, a hint of the exotic about him with his olive skin and hair so black it was almost blue. It was always a shock for the girls at first when they spoke to him to hear a broad Scottish accent coming from the lips of one they took to be a foreigner. Sandy was his opposite. He had the average height of a typical Scot, a nonde-script build, his hair was a pleasant light brown. Unremarkable really, except for his eyes which were blue, warm blue like a Scottish harebell, and a face that promised intelligence and kind-ness. His eyes crinkled when he laughed, which was often, and within minutes of meeting and talking to him, people were eager for his company.

CHAPTER 3

His family had weathered the war. There had been shortages but on the farm there was always enough food for everyone. The girls had grown, found suitors; a couple had now married and were expecting their own bairns. Aggie had brought another taste of the unknown into their lives when she introduced her beau, Major Bill Maclaren, one of the Canadian Air Force men posted to Scotland during the war. It was of him that Sandy and his elder brother William now talked as they shovelled coal from the coalman's cart into the cellar.

"What do you think of him then?" queried Sandy. "You've seen more of him than I have. Mother's all of a dither about it. Seems to be pleased with the man but horrified with the fact that he's foreign and will no doubt, if his intentions are honourable, want to take Aggie to Canada when they wed."

"Oh he's a decent enough man. I like him," replied William. "But why can't Aggie settle for one of the few who are interested in her from around here? These Canadians have got all the local girls in a whirl, what with their funny accents and their ready money."

"Sounds like a touch of sour grapes to me," quipped Sandy, digging his brother in the ribs and causing him to lose his shovelful of coal. "I think its great, as long as the man passes muster, and you all seem to think he does. You know..." He paused, setting down his spade, leaning on it thoughtfully. "I've a notion for Canada myself."

William looked hard at him. "What do you mean, you've a notion for Canada? What do you know about the place? It's the other side of the world!"

"Hardly," laughed Sandy, "but I'll grant you it's a fair distance. Still, think of what can be achieved in such a new country where everything's for the taking for someone with a bit of guts and not afraid of hard work and rough living. I heard about it – the fur trade actually – from someone in the Army and I'm sorely tempted. I'm going to make enquiries and I'll let you know what I find out. You might even be interested yourself."

"Why would I be interested?" snorted William. "And what's got into you? You're hardly back from bloody Africa and already you're talking about somewhere else foreign. What's wrong with Scotland? If you ask me, Sandy, the grass is always greener somewhere else for you."

"Maybe, maybe," mused Sandy, a faraway look in his eye. "But think, man, of the opportunities. And think what the prospects are here, stuck in some dead end job, seeing the same people with the same narrow views, with nothing more ambitious than a trip to Edinburgh on their horizons. Mark my words, Will, if you've got the courage, the world is at your feet!" He finished with a dramatic gesture at the grey Scottish sky already dark with the onset of night.

"There was always too much of the adventurer in you," muttered his brother. "Leave the travelling to our Aggie. We're needed here at home."

But there was a note of regret in his voice, thought Sandy as they continued their work in silence. *It wouldn't surprise me*, he pondered, *if he shows more than a token interest when I find out about the fur trading.*

CHAPTER 4

William swung his empty dinner pail over his shoulder. He was bone-weary after a ten-hour shift at the jute factory but already the fatigue was ebbing away at the thought of meeting Marie for the dance tonight. In fact he had better hurry. It was already past six o'clock and he had to get home, wash and change and then pick her up at the back of eight. Her lodgings were a good twenty-minute walk away from his house. He quickened his step, anticipating a hold-up at home as his brothers and his father queued up at the kitchen sink, all eager to wash off the day's grime before sitting down to their dinner, or anxious to get out to their evening's entertainment. Sandy would no doubt be off somewhere with his best mate Dom. About time those two men-about-town settled down instead of playing the field with half of the eligible young women of Carnoustie! And David, his other brother, would be off out with his young lady, a worthy sort, acknowledged William, but nothing, nothing at all compared to his Marie. The tantalising thought of her put a spring into his step and he began to whistle.

He could still hardly believe she was interested in him. He had met her when she had brought a group of excited chattering children around the jute mill – for a "look-see", William was told by his supervisor. Get them interested, they've a couple more years at school then they'll be after jobs and we want the cream of the crop. Well, he had no idea if his tour of the mill had fired up the imagination of those kids. He very much doubted it but there were worse jobs and for someone like himself, who hadn't the advantage of the education his family had been able to afford only for Sandy, it was a steady, reasonably paid job which, he had been led to believe, had possibilities. A foreman's position could be in the offing.

And my goodness, Marie had certainly fired up his imagination! She had breezed into the factory, surrounded by the kids, and that voluptuous figure, the toss of that blonde shingled head, and the flash of those bold, shining, intelligent eyes had quietened the endless, ear-splitting racket that was a feature of life on the factory floor. The workers' chatter continued, but all eyes and conversation were on Marie, one hundred and fifty males admiring and, he had no doubt, lusting after this very striking and confident young lady. And he had the job of showing her round! He was tongue-tied at first but she made it easy and the kids' boisterousness helped things. By the end of the tour, encouraged by her obvious interest in him, William had plucked up the courage to ask her out. And here he was, quite a few dates down the road and already planning to ask her to be his wife.

But something was different that night. William knew as soon as he picked her up that she was at first preoccupied and then apparently bored by the dance, by him, by his attentions. She seemed restless. She either ignored his attempts at conversation, her eyes constantly searching the room for something or someone more interesting, or she put him down, contradicting or dismissing, making him feel small and stupid. She had been this way before but never as rude or unfeeling. And because she was a schoolteacher, because she let him know on many occasions that she was infinitely superior in education and breeding, he suffered her scorn, telling himself he was the luckiest man alive just to be able to hold her in his arms on the dance floor. It was just a bad night, he told himself, maybe something to do with a woman's time of the month. He should know, he had enough sisters to be aware of how prickly they could become at times.

But when he took her home, his heart sank as she whisked herself out of his embrace before even his goodnight kiss and, without a backward glance or a promise of another meeting, slammed the door behind her.

CHAPTER 5

Nothing could have prepared William for the scene that greeted him a week later when he arrived back at home after work. It had been a tense, unhappy week with Marie. She had broken two dates with him, offering no explanation and certainly no remorse. The one outing they'd had together had been fraught with tension, he wondering if he ought to press for some reason for her change in attitude towards him but afraid of her reaction, and she highly-strung, off-hand to the point of rudeness. There had also been unpleasantness at work. A few of the men on the factory floor had made remarks in which her name featured, lewd remarks suggesting she could be anyone's if they had enough money to show her the high life. One glare from William had silenced them, but only for a moment and he soon became aware of whispered conversations, surreptitious glances in his direction. It was just jealousy, he told himself. They all wanted her, he knew that, but he had her and it was in the nature of some men to denigrate the unattainable.

And then the storm broke. The whole family except for Sandy and David, who were both still at work, was assembled in the farmhouse kitchen, mother in tears, father pacing in bewildered anger back and forward across the slate floor, thumping one fist into the other. As William entered the room, his mother let out a cry of anguish and flung herself into the arms of one of her daughters while father bellowed at him, disgust and rage thickening his words.

"What have you done, man? What in Heaven's name have you done?"

William looked at them all in alarm and fear. "I don't know what you're talking about. What do you mean, what have I done? Nothing, nothing as far as I know. What's the matter? Why is everyone crying? Why are you all here?"

"Don't give me that innocent rubbish!" his father roared. "You know too well the shame you've brought upon us. Look what you've done to your mother! She'll never be able to look others in the eye again!"

At that William's temper broke. It was the culmination of a week of misery and uncertainty. Work had been hard and uncomfortable, Marie had been impossible and now even those at home were accusing him of some horror so awful it had bound the family against him.

"If no one will tell me what's happened, I'm leaving!" he hissed and made as if to walk out through the door.

His words had their effect. His father sank to a chair and motioned for William to do the same. Mother's sobs softened and the girls stood in a terrible stillness.

"She's been here, your Marie." The quiet dejection in his father's voice made even more of an impression on William than his previous anger and he tensed himself, dreading what was to come next.

"She told us about the baby. That you took her, against her will, that she cannot keep this baby because she has no love or respect for you, that she's leaving here to go where no one will find her to wait out her term and then have the baby – our grandchild" – his voice broke on the word "– adopted".

The colour drained from William's face and he sat stunned into silence while he digested this information. His mother, convinced his silence was an admission of guilt, broke into further paroxysms of grief. Eventually he took a deep breath to control his voice and began to speak.

"It's all a lie. A wicked horrible lie. But it makes sense now," he mused almost to himself. "It makes monstrous sense and I hadn't the brains to see it before, blinded as I was with love and lust, I suppose." His mother took a sharp intake of breath at the word while his father sat grim-faced, awaiting William's explanation.

"She may be pregnant. From the rumours I've heard on the shop floor, any number of fine gentlemen could be the father. She was, apparently, very free with her favours if they were bought with presents and meals and perhaps even the merest suggestion of a permanent attachment to some toff or other who took a fancy to her. But of course I chose not to listen. My Marie, my clever, beautiful, CHASTE!" – he bellowed out the last word to the assembled company – "Marie. I never laid an inappropriate finger on her. I wanted to wait until she was my wife, you see. And now she's taken me for a patsy again. Silly besotted William, he'll take the blame." He laughed, a sharp bark of derision for himself and then suddenly asked: "But why come here to tell you these lies? What good would it do her to spin her wicked stories to you?"

"What good?!" His father was on his feet again. "To ask for money, of course. To take everything we had put by, to care for her until she gave birth to our grandchild. We begged her to reconsider. We said whatever wrong you had done her could be righted. You would marry her, we know you love her, and we would all help in bringing up the child. But she wouldn't listen. She was distraught, she wanted to be gone, so we gave her the money and we still hope that when her time comes maybe she'll change her mind and come back to you with the child."

"You don't believe me, do you?" William whispered. "How can you take her word against mine? Has her beauty addled your brains, as it did mine?" he added grimly. He waited, hoping for a denial but all around him were the shocked and disbelieving faces of his family.

"You have given me your answer," he said at last, "and I'm sorry. I'm sorry that you've handed over your money to a cheating, selfish bitch. I'm sorry you think so little of me that you choose to think the worst, and I'm particularly sorry that, because of this, I can't live here any longer. I'm leaving – now. I don't know where I'll go, probably Canada, but I'll let you know where I am when I get there. And I'll send you the money you so readily parted with. God, she really knew the family to pick, didn't she? I bet she couldn't believe her luck when she found you were all as gullible as me."

It took him only minutes to throw some clothes into a knapsack. They were still assembled in the kitchen when he came downstairs, a pathetic tableau, tears in the eyes of the women, an unhappy bewilderment on the face of his father. He gave his mother a quick kiss and then, terrified he would lose his courage if he faltered, he left the house without a backward look, panic and fear of the unknown taking the place of his anger.

CHAPTER 6

It was not long after William's departure that the sisters began again. Shocked by the drama, by the loss of one brother, they started their conspiracy to control Sandy. Initially they watched and waited, sizing up their baby brother. It took time. There were setbacks when they tried to push too quickly but gradually Sandy dropped his guard. The steel determination he had learned in the Army softened. He was no longer an individual but part of a bigger, more demanding unit – his family. He lived with them, shared their hopes and happiness; it was only fair he shared himself with them.

They niggled away gently at first. Why didn't he ask for a rise at the firm? He was well thought of, he was worth double what they were paying him, he really ought to be putting something by for a wife, a family of his own.

The first alarm bells began to ring and Sandy felt the silken ropes tighten. Aggie and Jan were the most insistent. Nearest to him in age, they felt a special relationship with him. They wanted to see him settled. Aggie was making her own plans to marry. Major Bill had asked her and, with excitement and a great deal of trepidation she was preparing to sail to Canada to be his bride. She wanted her little brother to be equally happy and that, as far as she was concerned, meant meeting the right girl and settling down. She was determined to "help" him in this objective before she left. As time ran out, so her nagging became unsupportable.

It was the Canadian connection that jogged Sandy's memory of the Company and the possibilities of another escape. He had seen an advertisement in the Dundee Courier: *"The opportunity of a lifetime with the Hudson's Bay Company, the oldest chartered trading company, offers a challenging career for young men. Applicants must be physically fit, unmarried, with the normal standard of education, and interested in learning merchandising, store operating and fur trading. Self-reliant, ambitious young men are wanted to work and live in small communities in Northern Canada."* Yes, this was the company his Army friend had mentioned to him.

It was worth a try. But thousands had applied, and they had their quota for the year. He had left it too late, and another year would have to pass before the interviewing started again. Sensing his disappointment and feeling an instant empathy with the young man, the recruiting officer beckoned Sandy back.

"I shouldn't be telling you this, but there's another company, a French outfit. Revillion Freres, competitors of ours. They seem to recruit all year round. I get the feeling you can't wait another year to get away. Pity, we could use men like you. But if you joined them you could always switch at a later date, and the experience you gained in the meantime would stand you in good stead. They operate out of Montreal."

Armed with the address and a reassurance that fluency in French was not a necessity, Sandy returned home and wrote and sent off the letter. *Better not tell the girls just yet*, he thought.

CHAPTER 7

He was called for interview to Glasgow and thereafter progress was startlingly quick. A doctor's note verifying his physical fitness was demanded and no sooner was this obtained when a letter containing a contract of employment arrived. All he had to do was sign.

There was no putting off telling the family. It was grim, worse than he had imagined. There was silence at first as the letter telling of his terms and conditions was passed from hand to hand. Mother, white-faced and near to tears, was the first to speak.

"It says you'll be gone two years Sandy! *Two years*! Have you not had enough of foreign parts? All that time in Africa away from us and now it's to be Canada! Just like William. You won't come back either." Her voice started to rise with her panic and emotion. "You're twenty-eight, Sandy! Where will you meet a suitable wife out there?"

His father interrupted abruptly, his voice rough with anger and the distress he shared with his wife.

"He couldn't afford to keep a wife on these wages! It's barely half what you're getting at Anderson-Grice. What's possessed you, man? Are we not good enough for you, is Scotland too safe, too small, too predictable after all your adventures? Och –" he sank into his seat, frustrated and uncomprehending "– what's the use? He'll go his own way as usual, whatever we say."

Stung at last to response, Sandy blurted, "I don't know why you're taking it all so personally. Of course I don't want to leave you all," he faltered slightly as he told the white lie, "but yes, I have got a taste for adventure. I do want to see more of the world, can't you understand I need broader horizons, different challenges? And you know this is not the same as William. He went off in a temper without thinking anything through, probably with little notion of where he'd end up. I'll be with a company, a good company who'll pay my fare there and back again." He emphasised the last two words. "I know the money's poor at the moment but it's only until I complete my training. And don't forget, it's practically all pocket money. I'm fed, clothed and housed. What more do I need?"

He paused, taking his eyes off his mother and father briefly to look at his brother and sisters who clustered in the background. The girls were tearful. Jan stood with her arm around Aggie as her sister wiped her eyes with her apron, but Sandy could see a faint smirk of satisfaction in the countenance of his brother David. He couldn't blame him. It must be a novel and welcoming experience for David to watch his parents' favourite son being questioned and criticised. *I'm doing him a favour really by leaving,* he thought.

"And as for a wife," he continued, "that's the last thing on my mind. Oh, I know," he held up his hand as his mother drew breath to intervene: "I did have a notion of Nancy Docherty last spring but that's all it was, a notion. And the relief was unexpected but immense when she got tired of waiting for me and married Cameron MacDonald. You've got the rest of your daughters to wed, Mother, and there's Mima and Jean about to give birth. You'll have more grand-bairns than you know what to do with without me adding to the list." He grinned, his good humour restored and as always his mother responded to his charm, already compliant to his wishes and briefly confident in his optimism.

"Ah well, as your father says, you will have it your own way. And," she brightened as a thought struck her, "you'll be near Aggie and Bill. He's a good man but it'll make such a difference having you at hand should she find Canada strange at first, when she gets there."

Brother and sister exchanged glances and they both smiled

at their mother. She had no comprehension of the vastness of this country to which they were both travelling. She did not realise that she, in Scotland, would be as close to her daughter in Prince Edward Isle as Sandy would be in the far north-west Quebec province at Port Harrison. If it gave her comfort to imagine them near to each other, then they would not enlighten her.

The family meeting broke up and Sandy sighed quietly with relief. The first hurdle, the main one really, was over. There would be more tears and emotional blackmail as his departure date drew nearer, painful for him as for them. But, he allowed himself a moment of drama as he struck a mental pose. The die was cast. *Canada, here I come.*

The small room he shared now only with his brother David since William had left so dramatically seemed strangely both comforting and claustrophobic. Sandy knew he needed to shed himself of physical and mental restrictions before his home and the town became his only horizons, robbing him of imagination and ambition. It would be so easy to settle as he was now, cosy and warm in the feather bed that would become his life if he stayed. Known and liked in the neighbourhood, on a steady if gradual ladder of success in the engineering firm, it was an enviable scenario. What if Nancy had waited for him! He trembled involuntarily at the picture that thought painted in his mind's eye. A bonnie girl but not for him. No challenge, a settling for mediocrity, safety and before he knew it there would be a mortgage, bairns.

He wondered introspectively why such a prospect filled him with horror. Nine out of ten people would welcome such a future, delighted that they had the excellent prospects he commanded. Why was he so different? But then there was William who had walked into the unknown without a second thought, and even Aggie who was preparing to leave behind her all that was dear and familiar to join a relative stranger in his foreign land and culture. Pretty impressive for one family, he reflected, suddenly assured of the rightness of his decision. Again, aware of his fondness for the dramatic, he saw himself in the pioneering footsteps of such great Scots as David Livingstone. He chuckled then at his own inflated opinion of himself. Dozens, hundreds probably, of young Scots had preceded him, at a much younger age and without his own invaluable experience of life abroad, to join the ranks of the employees of the great fur-trading companies. A pioneer indeed! He might overawe the majority of the citizens in this modest coastal town with his daring, but he would shortly be sharing his life with men who had taken this step he was about to make when pioneering really was the name of the game.

Later, in the musing time between waking and sleeping, Sandy reviewed his decision. He should have known that his brother would be mentioned now, although his name had not been spoken in the house since he had walked out two years ago without a backward glance, a rucksack of belongings slung over his shoulder. The door had slammed behind William, leaving a family shocked, angry but afraid of what the future would hold for him.

What had happened to him? He'd said he was going to Canada but where and to do what? William, the apple of his mother's eye – a position Sandy knew he had inherited, rightly or wrongly. But Sandy's departure would be different. He now had his parents' blessing and he would write to them, let them share, at a distance, his new life.

Most importantly, he would come home.

CHAPTER 8

Their voices droned on and on and every word jarred his senses. He looked outwardly docile and obedient as they paced the dark drawing room in front of him. His face was impassive, giving no indication of his reaction to their demands. Nothing had changed. It was as though the last two years had never happened. Sandy corrected himself. On a purely economic level, certain things *had* changed. There was more money to share now that the family had grown and the girls were either married or supporting themselves. There was a middle-class feel to the farmhouse that had not existed before and the girls had taken elocution lessons with dubious success, their Scottish accents now overtoned with uncomfortable attempts at polite pronunciation. Jan, finally resigned to her spinster state, had become even more bitter and domineering; Jean, a mother with a small baby and a weak excuse of a man for a husband, had become an alarming copy of her elder sister. Two bossy, opinionated women who were convinced they had his best interests at heart and would brook no argument.

Jan, her voice as harsh and severe as her appearance, paused in mid-sentence and peered in his direction through the gloom.

"Are you paying attention Sandy? I would have expected some contribution from you by now."

"Give him time." Jean's tone was deceptively soothing. She tended to get her way through repetitive persuasion rather than direct demands, but she invariably got it. "We've only just sprung it on him. He'll need a moment to realise how right this is for him."

And they were off again, discussing his future as though he were hardly there, as though his presence or his opinion was a matter of no consequence. They had already decided. Telling him was just a formality. The room was stifling. The heavy maroon velvet curtains were tightly closed although it was only late afternoon and the weak sunshine still dappled the gravel drive outside. The curtains were always drawn in this room, to prevent the dark red carpet from fading. Heavy mahogany furniture, more than he remembered, filled every space. Perhaps as the children had left their nest, his parents had peopled the rooms with inanimate objects to fill their lives and now every movement in this room was an obstacle course. Occasional tables, overstuffed sofas, dreary drooping plants wilting from the heat and lack of light cast shadows and a curious melancholy over the scene. A coal fire spluttered and spat nuggets of coke into the grate. Sandy was suddenly claustrophobic, hemmed in by their words, the heat, the stiff unbending formality of the room.

But he owed them his attention. He had made his escape two years ago and it had been the right choice, the best move of his life. And it was a permanent escape, for after these few months of furlough he would return to Port Harrison to the life that pleased and suited him like no other. Then these sisters would have to turn again to each other to bully and organise. He could cope with their undivided attention for this short time. Besides, he found, to his astonishment, that he was beginning to show interest in their plans. They were starting to make sense, he could see and perhaps even agree with their logic. Careful, he warned himself. Listen, assess and then decide.

Jan was holding forth again. "She's from a very good family, the Richardsons, moved from Dundee. Her father John Richardson is the manager of the Bank of Scotland in Carnoustie. He took up the post shortly after you left, established himself quickly and is well thought of. The girl herself, Ella, is a pleasant creature, biddable, and at her age realises that marriage prospects are fading fast so there should be no difficulty with the fact that you'll be whisking her off to Canada the minute you're married. Aggie has settled well there with Bill.

There's no reason why she shouldn't take to it as well."

Sandy winced imperceptibly as he saw Jan's face tighten when she mentioned the girl's age and lack of offers. *She still regrets her own single state*, he thought. Jan had lost her fiancé in the trenches in Belgium and such was her grief that her once pretty face had aged into a mask of harsh lines and frowns. Her acerbic tongue had frightened off the most determined of suitors and when at last her mourning was over, it was too late. Her fearsome reputation and sour demeanour were too well established to tempt any man to court her. Sandy wondered what had kept the Richardson girl from the altar; maybe a similar loss in the war. At twenty-eight she was old for a prospective bride and if Jan approved of her, maybe she too was a shrew. No. Jan would favour someone mild, timid. Opposites attract and Jan would approve of her while at the same time faintly despising a tractable character weaker than her own.

Jean had now taken over the monologue while Jan stoked the coals, sending out further unnecessary flames. The two women, clothed in thick drab dresses of worsted and clutching woollen shawls about their shoulders, seemed impervious to the stifling atmosphere while Sandy could feel the sweat cluster damply round his armpits, trickle down his chest and form wet patches behind his knees, around his groin and in the sticky darkness of his boots. His face felt on fire.

"We've been invited to dinner, Friday seven o'clock. I trust you'll go with an open mind, Sandy, and not too many stories about the place you've come from. No doubt they're wildly exaggerated. Aggie doesn't tell of weather like that, and we don't want to frighten the girl, do we? Oh, and not too much of the whisky either. Your face goes like a boiled lobster, most unattractive. Just stick to wine. Well, that's settled now." Jean rubbed her hands together with satisfaction and beamed at Jan. "I think this young brother of ours has a lot to thank us for."

The briefing was over and in spite of himself, Sandy was intrigued. A wife. It might not be a bad idea. It would depend heavily upon the girl, of course. He laughed to himself as he reviewed his sisters' idea of the Canada he had lived in for the past two years. Not the mild temperate climate of Prince Edward Island, where Aggie and Bill lived, but the wild heart-stopping cold of the Arctic, unimaginable to those who had not experienced it first hand.

They still had no concept of the hugeness of this country. His mother had even quietly taken him aside and asked if he had seen or heard of William while he was there. As though he were liable to bump into him around the next corner! There were no corners where Sandy had been living. Very little besides wilderness and sea, snow and ice, just south of the Arctic tundra on the furthermost edge of the tree line. It took courage to live there and although it suited him, a woman would find it a very different proposition. Still, he would meet her without prejudice and with her suitability hopefully in his mind.

He was unsure why this wife notion had taken root at all in his mind. He had entertained and rejected the idea on numerous occasions when his sisters had set off on their usual tack. There had always been reasons, valid or simply convenient excuses which he had employed to defend himself from their attacks. Why was it different this time? Surely nothing as mundane as them wearing him out, the last straw syndrome? No, that was not in his character. If anything, he became more obstinate when bombarded. It must be something deep inside himself that had been growing without his being consciously aware of it. A need, an emptiness perhaps that he had not identified until now. He had thought his life was full, satisfying and yet... He knew he enjoyed the reflected warmth he experienced when he was around a happy family. That was part of the attraction the Eskimo people held for him. Their family life was, almost without exception, idyllic. Deprived of almost every comfort, living from year to year with starvation and death an ever present threat, they nevertheless lived happy lives, secure in the close bonding and love that existed between them. Husband and wife respected each other and the children were adored and spoiled by all.

Sandy was not aware he had envied them, but it was now obvious to him that an idea had been growing imperceptibly, a sense of "why not me?", and his sisters had at last, by chance, struck at the right moment. Friday would be interesting.

CHAPTER 9

William breathed in deeply, savouring the smell of the pine forest around him and revelling in the loveliness of the day. He laughed inwardly at himself, that something as simple as a lush meadow, as the overhanging sweep of a fragrant bough and the brush of the pine needle against his cheek, could today give him such sharp pleasure when he had experienced all this so many times before without giving it another thought. But there was a good feeling about this day and William paid attention to his intuitions. He was looking forward to doing business again with Koosees. The Cree chief had traded with him a number of times and his furs were always of the highest quality. But there was more to it than that. They respected each other, enjoyed each other's company. Koosees ran a tight camp, his braves were intelligent and hard-working and the fruit of their labours throughout the autumn and winter were the beautiful pelts that they would offer first to William, knowing he would honour their industry and give them a fair price for the skins.

How right he had been to leave the railroad, he thought as he trudged through the forest towards the Cree summer camp. How right he had been to leave Scotland. But that was a memory that was foolish to visit on such a day as this; when he wanted to cling to this feeling of euphoria and not sully it with thoughts that upset and angered. Nevertheless, he allowed his mind to wander, back to the days on board the ship that had brought him here to Canada, back to the men he had met there who had encouraged him to go with them to the building of the mighty railway which wound its way westward through Ontario. It had been a good time in its way, he mused. It had given him breathing space to acclimatise, to adapt to this country, to learn its ways and realise its potential. He had made friends, the hard repetitive work had toughened his body and he had, with little effort, amassed a nest-egg, giving him options to a future that suited him more than the monotony of the unskilled labour which the "fire sleigh trail", the railway in Cree Indian terms, demanded of him. William smiled to himself and bent down to pat one of the six husky dogs that gambolled about his feet, all of them enjoying the day and the walk as much as he.

"And that's when I got you lot, isn't it?" he said out loud to the dogs who, encouraged by his voice and interest, jumped up at him, their tongues lolling and with silly grins on their faces. "And off we went, scouring the west coast of James Bay for the furs the ladies of the world are crying out for, white and silver fox, beaver, wolf, seal. And haven't we done well, boys, haven't we done well! Of course you have the most intelligent of masters. I hope you realise that. Who would have thought a simple worker from the jute mills of Dundee could master the Cree language and because of that and my natural affability – you know what an amiable fellow I am, don't you! – gain their trust and respect and have my pick of the best skins in the area. Perhaps the fact that I can offer them five dollars a pelt more than the big companies, low overheads," he laughed as he rattled the dismantled tent he kept in a hide roll slung over his shoulder, "could have had a bearing on our success. But I prefer to think it's my natural charm they fell for. What do you say, boys?"

He carried on his banter with the dogs until they came to the clearing in which, by the side of the broad sweep of the Eastmain River, the camp of Koosees was pitched. The chief made known his pleasure in his greeting to William. His two sons, of a similar age to the young Scot, were equally pleased to meet the trader and had even taken him with them on occasions when they laid their traps for the pine marten and the fox. This year their winter catch had been magnificent.

CHAPTER 10

The furs were beautiful, the finest William had seen, sixty-eight marten skin, all a rich dark fur that would command a top price when he sold on. His business with the chief concluded, William was euphoric.

"Stay, eat with us," urged Koosees. "We are lucky. Today we caught the first of the blue geese. My daughter Kunee has been roasting the bird and you will share our feast." The *wavy*, an anglicization of the Cree word *waywao*, was a particular delicacy and a surprising one at this time, as the geese started their migration in the autumn. In this case the unlucky early bird, thought William, but needed no further persuasion to join his friends.

It was then that William noticed for the first time the graceful figure of the girl as she knelt by the fire, turning the spit and basting the bird with its own juices. The unexpected force of her beauty struck him like a blow. He found himself breathless and tongue-tied, able only to accept Koosees' invitation with a gesture and a smile. Later, as they sat around the campfire replete with the delicious meat of the goose, he found it hard to concentrate on the hunting talk between the men of the settlement. There was a silence and William realised a question had been directed at him. All eyes were on him and Koosees was laughing.

"You wish to speak with my daughter. Go. Our business is finished. Now make sweet talk. She wishes it. She has seen you here before. Why do you think I save the marten pelts for you!"

The men roared with laughter at the look of amazement on his face. Red-faced and bewildered, William stumbled awkwardly to his feet and, mumbling his thanks, shuffled hesitantly out of the light of the fire and into the darker shadows left by the tents where he knew Kunee sat smiling at him. She motioned him to sit and to his further amazement began to speak to him in English.

"I am glad you came to us today. My father is happy to trade with you. He knows you are an honourable man who will give him a fair price for his furs. He is the finest trapper in our settlement. He will bring you many furs and you will visit often. Then I will talk with you and you will tell me many things I wish to know of your country."

A wave of such intense feeling swept over him as he looked into her lovely face, her skin smooth and young, her eyes black and shining in the moonlight. Her thick lustrous hair swung like a velvet curtain towards him as she bent closer to him, anxious to hear him agree to her words.

"Yes," he managed at last, "yes, I should like that."

They talked well into the night in low murmurs as the others unrolled their bed-rolls and one by one settled down to sleep. Still bemused by her beauty, her interest in him and by this new and frightening emotion he was experiencing William was hesitant at first, answering only her questions and volunteering little himself. The spell lifted as she urged him to tell her of his home, of Scotland and the life he had left behind. Abruptly, reality forced its way into his consciousness and he turned from her gruffly.

"That is something of which I cannot speak."

Hurt by the coldness of his voice, her eyes clouded and she withdrew the slim hand that had been resting within his.

"Maybe later, Kunee," he added quickly, anxious to recapture the tenderness of the past few hours with her. "It's just too soon. There are things which I will tell you in time. I want you to know me better before you are forced to pass judgement on me as they did," he whispered almost to himself.

But she caught his mood and his fear and was content to let him have his way. She had chosen this man for herself. Unobserved, she had watched him on the two previous occasions he had traded with her father and with a certainty born not only from the physical thrill she had felt at the sight of this tall hand-some white man but from an almost spiritual knowledge of their rightness for each other, she knew that whatever he told her would make no difference to her love for him. She would wait until he was ready. She took his hand again and smiled.

"It will be good, William," she promised.

CHAPTER 11

Their love affair progressed throughout the summer and William spent his days away from Kunee in a fever of longing for their next meeting. As autumn approached he knew he must make his decision. She would disappear with her family into the forests of the hinterland, the snow would come, the rivers and the lakes would freeze over and she would be hidden from William until the spring and their return to the summer camp. Already Koosees had visited the Hudson's Bay post to buy, with the dollars William had paid him for the furs they had traded and with an advance from the company, the merchandise and ammunition he needed for the winter isolation.

They stood surrounded by the cases of ammunition, fish nets and twine, steel traps, tea, sugar, salt and tobacco. The family's needs were modest. The forests would provide the wood for their tepee and their campfires; fish, black bear, moose would feed them and the pelts of the fur-bearing animals would be at their richest and glossiest, ensuring a healthy trade for the following spring. But the winters could be cruel. There were times of scarcity and sometimes starvation threatened.

"I can't let you go," he blurted out at last, holding Kunee's hands so tightly she winced involuntarily at the pressure. She looked so small and vulnerable to him. She needed him to take care of her, provide for her, he persuaded himself, although he knew in reality it was his weakness, his need of her that shaped and clarified his decision.

"And now I have to tell you what you wanted to know when we first met. There must be no secrets between us." His voice heavy with reluctance, he dragged the story from deep within himself where he had buried it to ease his pain.

"I was in love once before. Her name was Marie. A bonny thing, intelligent too, a schoolteacher. I couldn't believe my luck – that she had chosen me. I had no money, no looks, I was a very poor prospect for one such as her. But I seemed to fit the bill at the time and I was getting up the courage to ask her to marry me once I had a promotion at work. They'd told me there was one in the offing," he explained.

"And then she changed. She'd break a date without a proper explanation. She seemed to be thinking of other things when we were together, wanting to be somewhere else, with someone else. At least that's the impression I got but I kept telling myself I was imagining it all. One of my friends tried telling me there were rumours about her, nasty things about her reputation as a fast piece, a gold digger, but of course I didn't listen. I thought it was jealousy, sour grapes. If she were a gold digger then what was she doing with me? I reasoned.

"What indeed! Safe dependable William, always around to take her out when she was at a loose end, when her other fancy men weren't available. The sort of men she set her cap at, wealthy men-about-town with their flashy cars and full wallets, were happy enough to wine and dine her and bed her but would run a mile when they saw she was interested in a more permanent arrangement. Oh no, marriage wasn't on the cards for any of them. Then she found she was pregnant. She probably didn't even know for sure who the father was but they all denied responsibility, melted away like snow off a dyke. And pretty, frightened Marie played the only hand left to her. She went to my parents and said I was to blame."

Kunee drew in her breath and made to speak but William stopped her. "Not yet please. If I don't get this told all at once I might never get it done. Well," he continued, "they fell for it. My parents actually fell for it. It was a lie, of course. I never touched her that way. I wanted to. She drove me mad with desire. I think she probably wouldn't have minded if I had tried it on. But I had been brought up to respect a girl, to know it was wrong to give in to temptation. And I planned to marry her after all, so I knew I could wait for her, that in the end she would be mine. What an idiot! What a stupid naïve idiot!

"I was still at work when she went round to the house. She had planned it that way, of course. She burst into tears, told my parents that I'd 'had my evil way with her' – against her will, she said! – and she was now pregnant. She would have the baby but she didn't want to keep it. She would put it up for adoption. She didn't love me, so marriage was out of the question. And because she couldn't stay in Dundee, for all the world to see her shame, she would have to leave her job, her very well paid job (she told them), and go elsewhere until she had the baby. And for that she would need money. She thought they ought to know the facts and she was sure they would want to help her under the circumstances.

"When I came home she was long gone with all the money the family could spare and I was met by their anger, their disappointment, their disgust – oh, you name it, I was the devil's own, to hear them speak. I denied it, over and over again I told them it was all lies, but no one listened and in the end I just gave up, packed my bag and left. They believed her rather than me, the son they had brought up to tell the truth and to live by their strict moral standards." He shook his head. " I still find it amazing, after all this time, how easily she charmed them. The men, my father, my two brothers, could see the temptation she had been. Naturally I had given in to it. But my sisters, my mother, how could they not see through her? I couldn't live with that. I felt they had betrayed me, all of them. They had thrown away all those years of trust and love and I couldn't live with that knowledge. So I had to leave. And that's what brought me to Canada," he finished lamely.

Kunee cradled his head in her arms, her heart crying for him in his distress.

"I love you William," she whispered, "and I will stay with you always. Before the tribe depart we will be married, with the blessing of my family. We will share the winter together and one day, when our love has driven out all your pain, you will be able to forgive those who have wronged you and thank them for sending you to me."

CHAPTER 12

Sandy told Dom about the dinner party the following day. They had met at the Carnoustie Golf Club, played eighteen holes with the usual unequal mixture of frustration and deep satisfaction and now, relaxed and comfortable with their single malts in front of them, they discussed Sandy's future.

It had been so easy to take up with his friend again, thought Sandy. Just as it had been after the war, it was as though the years separating them had never happened, although significant changes had occurred in both their lives. Dom had married Maria, a tiny vivacious distant cousin who had come for a brief visit and had only returned to Italy to collect her trousseau and her family for a splendid wedding in Dundee. The local girls had mourned for days at the loss of this most eligible of bachelors and then had turned their attentions to the next one on their list. Dom was now a respectable married man with an exquisite doll-like baby daughter and a comfortable living as head of the family business. It was a life so removed from Sandy's as to render their compatibility almost impossible. But their friendship was firm and Dom found his adventure in Sandy's tales of Canada and the fur trade. His happy but ordinary life was enriched by the exotic life of his friend. Neither envied the other but instead enjoyed their differences.

"Go on," Dom urged as Sandy paused to sip his whisky. He smiled as the golden liquid warmed and comforted him.

"You know the family, of course?"

"Of course. The parents, that is, and not well. We don't bank with him but since they moved from Dundee they've made their mark. The father, John Richardson, is already on the board of the chamber of commerce and his wife's a leading light of the Women's Guild at St. Andrews. Needless to say we don't mix." He laughed wryly. "Too foreign, too Catholic! But don't get me wrong," he assured his friend, "they seem to be good people."

Sandy nodded slowly and thoughtfully. "I think so too."

The evening had gone well. The Richardson house, compared to Lunans' own, had been impressive and imposing. A carriage sent by the Richardsons for their convenience had deposited Sandy, his mother and father, Jan and Jean at the front door of the manor house. The long approach to the house, a drive bordered by flowering rhododendron bushes, had served to silence the two sisters, who had previously been chatting excitedly about the forthcoming evening. They had never visited Ella at her home before; their acquaintance and friendship with her, her mother and sister had been conducted entirely at meetings of the womans' fellowship at the church. Overawed and apprehensive, they glanced anxiously at Sandy, who took care to conceal his amusement at their discomposure. Once inside the house, however, their natural exuberance returned and the splendour of the manor house was purely an appendage to the genuine warmth of their welcome by the Richardsons.

Dinner was impressive. Course after course appeared accompanied by a variety of wines and sherries, port and brandies. The rooms glittered with the sparkle of light on fine glass, chandeliers, candlesticks, goblets, all of premium Edinburgh crystal. Silverware and heavy Irish linen enhanced the elegance of the dining room where every beautiful piece of furniture glowed with years of polish, care and attention. The drawing room was equally charming. Here, instead of the rich reddish brown of the mahogany furniture, walnut was favoured. Complemented by a gold and dark blue upholstery, the wood was perfect for the warm and tasteful opulence of the room. Paintings, mostly watercolours, Sandy observed, papered the walls but did not dominate, their subject matter restful lakes or woodland scenes, picked mainly, he surmised, for their colours rather than for any artistic merit. So there are flaws, Sandy thought with relief. All this perfection, beauty and elegance tempered by evidence of the mundane. It was reassuringly touching.

Dom sat back and stared hard at his friend. "You're beginning to alarm me, man, all this detail and still not a word…"

"I know," interrupted Sandy. "I think it's because I still haven't formed an opinion, even sorted out my thoughts. It was easy to set the scene, comment on the obvious, pat myself on the back because I wasn't seduced or fooled by the luxury."

"Yes, I understand that. But now I want to hear the important things. Talk your way through it, slowly. As though you were seeing her again for the first time."

Sandy nodded, sat in silence for a moment and then, his eyes focused on a point behind Dom's head, began to speak.

"She met us in the hall, and after her mother and father had welcomed us, the two sisters were introduced – Florence first and then, almost as though they were saving a special treat, Ella. Phew, what can I say?" He shook his head, searching for words. "She's plain, Dom, there's no two ways about it, she's plain. Not ugly, no warts or scars or birthmarks. Just – unremarkable." He stopped and looked for a reaction but Dom only waved his hand in a gesture of encouragement. "All right." The admission now made he appeared to find it easier to speak the words. "Her hair, brownish, a bit like mine I suppose." He laughed briefly. "She had it up, bun thing at the back, parted in the middle. Most unattractive yet they all seem to do it. A sort of pale pasty complexion, blueish eyes, I think. Oh dammit, everything about her seemed washed out, used up, if you know what I mean." He stopped in exasperation and then continued: "Her figure isn't much better. Stocky, the same up as down. I doubt there's a waist although you can't tell anything when they button themselves into yards of muddy-coloured cardigan." He stopped again, this time for so long Dom blurted out impatiently

"I take it there's more?"

"Yes, yes." Sandy spoke slowly, a note of pleasure now warmed his tone. "She has the loveliest voice, Dom. It's low and gentle. I can't really describe it. Musical, but that's an adjective that's practically meaningless. All I can say is, she suddenly became a person when she started to speak. Not this poor faded creature but someone you wanted to listen to, whose opinions you valued."

Dom threw himself back in his chair, a grin stretching his handsome face and all the tension he had been unaware of feeling flooded out of his limbs.

"And did she have many opinions?" he queried.

"Aye. Plenty! I tell you, that family have something to say about everything! I get the impression that between them, given time, they could set the world to right."

"But they were interested in you, surely? They didn't spend the whole evening discussing politics or banking or – whatever?" Dom leaned forward again, a worried frown on his face.

"I had the floor of the house practically the entire evening," Sandy announced with huge satisfaction. "They hung on my every word!"

He had indeed dominated the conversation. His sisters sat quietly hopeful, his parents, their pride in him obvious in their faces, faded into the background while Sandy hypnotised his audience with stories of a people and a climate so foreign as to be almost beyond their imagination. He spoke well. He told of white-outs, blizzards that blew so fiercely a man could become disorientated and die within yards of shelter. Of the huge white bear the Inuit called Nanuq. Of the people themselves, their skill as hunters, their courage in this forbidding climate and above all, their warmth as human beings. One of them, a mighty hunter widely respected by the people of the area, was also called Nanuq, a tribute to his strength and importance. Sandy had helped the filmmaker, Robert J. Flaherty, document a few days in the life of this exceptional Inuk and the resulting film, Nanook of the North, had generated international acclaim.

"I stopped occasionally," he confessed ingenuously, "to give someone else a chance to speak. But they would have none of it. They wanted more, she, Ella, particularly. Until I had to finish when my voice gave out!"

Dom finished his Glenfidditch and patted his friend on the back. "Well, we can safely say an impression has been made. But how about yourself? What happens next?"

"I'm taking her to the theatre this weekend."

CHAPTER 13

Ella collected her reticule and wrap from the seat next to her and allowed herself to be escorted by Sandy from the Kings Theatre. The entertainment had been enjoyable, a musical comedy, and they had laughed together. But throughout her thoughts had been focused on the man at her side.

She still felt uncomfortable in the unfamiliar brown velvet dress pressed upon her by her sister. It was startlingly stylish. The hemline fell just below her knees and she continually had to restrain herself from tugging it down to cover the nakedness of her legs – shapely legs, she had to admit to herself. She remembered the astonishment and pleasure she had felt at her reflection in the cheval glass in her bedroom. Her hair had been dressed differently, small curls teased out which framed and softened her face. A beautiful string of amber beads, her mother's, hung to her waist. The excitement of the occasion had brought a flattering pink glow to an otherwise sallow complexion. She looked a different person and the family's cries of admiration had only served to heighten her nervousness. Ella had never been the centre of attention. She was not sure that she welcomed this phenomenon, however brief the duration.

Sandy had not echoed their approval. His manners could not be faulted, everything done the way it should be. He had even brought her a corsage which flustered her further until her mother had taken charge and pinned it firmly to her coat. They had talked in the cab without awkwardness, however, and he had complimented her on her appearance. But there was no special look in his eye, no true admiration in his voice. *He's going through the motions*, she thought dully.

"I did think we might take supper at Wilson's." His voice startled her from her gloomy thoughts. " We still can if you'd like, I have a reservation. But I wondered, it's such a lovely evening, maybe a stroll around the park instead? I think the quietness and solitude would suit us better than a noisy restaurant."

A quick nod of her head signalled her agreement and as he took her arm and measured his step to match hers, she felt a stir of hope and excitement. The moonlight lit up their path. Other couples passed them, their heads close together, whispering intimately. Ella's spirits sank again. They, she and Sandy, looked so formal. They could have been brother and sister, although, she acknowledged sadly, there would have been more warmth between siblings. She searched frantically for conversation to hide her hurt and disappointment and was about to launch into a favourable critique of the play they had just seen when Sandy stopped and indicated that she should sit on a wrought iron bench by the side of a pond. She perched on the edge, feeling the metal cold through the layers of her clothes. The ducks were sleeping, their beaks tucked into their feathers. There was a distant hoot from an owl and a pleasing ripple from the water at their feet as it lapped against the grassy border. Otherwise there was silence.

Sandy sat beside her, took her hand and cleared his throat. "Ella. I know this is sudden but I have little time." He paused and his eyes held hers as she sat frozen with a mixture of terror, shock and anticipation. "Ella." He tried again. "Would you do me the honour of becoming my wife?"

He waited but Ella could only stare at him in fascinated disbelief, her hand rigid in his. Her eyes had become huge as they searched his face. Suddenly a wave of tenderness for her, her simplicity and the naked hope he read in her face relaxed him and allowed him to find the right words, the words she expected and deserved.

"We have met only twice but already I admire you more than any woman I have known. I feel comfortable in your company. I enjoy and respect your intelligence. I sense a per-

Aupaluktuk - the Red One

sonality compatible with my own, someone who would welcome a life-style uncomplicated by the worldly trappings of
so-called civilisation." He found, to his astonishment, that he
had spoken words he now knew he believed in. It made it
easier to continue.

"Ella, I cannot say I love you. I've never believed in the
notion of love at first sight. That love, I'm almost certain, is
confused with lust." At this Ella flinched, an instinctive reaction
to a word she thought disgusted her but which, paradoxically,
she wished Sandy felt about her. He was no longer looking at
her but seemed to be directing his speech at a spot beyond her,
speaking his thoughts aloud rather than communicating with
her. She was content to let him talk while a whirlwind of emotions raced through her mind.

"Our marriage would be based on friendship, which I'm
convinced in time would grow into love. Time together, experiences shared, hardships endured. And Ella, I must warn you,
there *will* be hardships." He was back with her again and an
urgency had entered his voice. "I fear I made my life in the
Arctic sound romantic and adventurous the other night. I
wanted to impress you and your family and the picture I painted
was a distortion of the truth. You must be aware of the life
I'm offering you, even the dangers it holds, before you give me
your answer. I would be doing us both a disservice if you were
misled."

And on he talked with serious intent but with an enthusiasm
he could not disguise. She was content to listen but much of it
she did not absorb. His warnings of the cold, of the primitive
conditions and the lack of contact with any but the alien people
he called the Inuit who he seemed to love excited rather than
frightened her. She knew her strengths, she was satisfied that he
too had recognised them and she was confident that she could
take anything in her stride with him beside her. But there would
be times when he could not be with her, he cautioned. When he
was absent from the base for days hunting, visiting his trappers,
attending to emergencies. These people expected his attention

and loyalty, the company demanded his wholehearted devotion to duty. Sometimes she would have to come second. The loneliness could be unbearable.

But she shrugged happily and, at last convinced he had set before her all the downsides to a life shared with him, he faltered to a stop. He was suddenly aware that she had not uttered a word since they had entered the park although the expressions he had read on her face seemed to speak for themselves.

"Forgive me, Ella. I've had my say, for too long I expect you're thinking. But it all had to be said and the opportunity was before me. I don't expect your answer yet. Think about it, discuss it with your sister, your mother and father. Ask me questions. But if it is as I hope and your answer will be yes, tell me soon. I'm anxious to take you back with me as my bride and there'll be much to arrange in a very short time."

Ella found her voice at last. "There's nothing to worry about or discuss, Sandy. I know now I'm happy to be your wife and to share the life that already gives you such satisfaction and fulfilment. I wonder that you feel I could enrich such a life but I'm anxious to prove you right."

For once at a loss for words and bemused by his unexpectedly rapid success, Sandy could only beam at her foolishly. A clock struck the hour. Eleven o'clock. They hurried back through the park, each pleased with the other and with the knowledge that their news would startle but hugely gratify their families. Florence would claim her brown velvet dress had caused the magic. Mother would fondle her precious beads smugly, thought Ella. But she knew Sandy liked the plain Ella best. The one to whom ornaments and pretty dresses were an irrelevance. She was the one he had decided would suit his life in the hostile wastes of the frozen northlands.

CHAPTER 14

The few weeks remaining of his leave flew by. There was so much to organize and after the initial gathering of the families to celebrate the engagement, Sandy and Ella saw little of each other. She had a wedding to prepare for, he all the logistics of their journey back to Port Harrison to plan. The company was pleased with his decision to marry. To his astonishment, his five-year apprenticeship had been cut short and although he had only served two years, he was appointed post manager. This, he was led to understand, was because he had learned quickly and well, had shown an aptitude and instinct for the job and above all had established a rapport with the Inuit. He was already respected and trusted. Now, with a wife and, in time, inevitably a family, he was considered a valuable asset to the company. He had done well.

Ella spent her time in a whirl of preparation. Dizzied by the heady new experience of being the centre of attention, she allowed herself to be ferried from dressmaker to florist, to bootmaker and furrier, minister and organist. Her family had thrown themselves into the organization of her wedding and her new life with an enthusiasm that left her grateful but bewildered. Cabin trunks were purchased and filled with astonishing speed. The creation of the wedding dress alone seemed to fill her days with a storm of paper patterns, swatches of material, pins, measures, interminable fittings and, in the end, disappointment as she realized, too late, that the ivory satin was a mistake, the colour muddying her complexion and its fluid shimmering lines revealing too cruelly the stockiness of her figure.

But she was happy. This was, after all, the most exciting time of her life. There had been one sobering moment, however, which worried away at the edge of her consciousness and caused her sleep to be filled with dark, hardly-remembered dreams of impending sadness. On one of his rare visits to her house, Sandy had stopped by a cabin trunk in the hall, its lid open to expose the white and gold beauty of her new dinner service. Servants were wrapping each exquisite piece with careful dedication, enjoying the delicate china as much as she had when she chose it. He had stood quietly for a moment and then looked up at her as she ran happily towards him, eager to hear his pleasure in their latest acquisition. His face had been thunderous and although he kept his voice low, there was a fury in it that she had never heard before.

"What's all of this?" he demanded.

"Why, the new dinner service my parents are giving us. Don't you like it? I can have it changed. I thought its very plainness would please you but we can choose again together – this afternoon…"

"Are you thinking of taking it with us?" he interrupted. "Are you really expecting to travel with fine china? Have you no concept of the house you will live in, the life you'll lead with me?" His voice rose and his grip on her tightened as he led her away from the astonished servants and into the empty drawing room. Realising now from the look of panic on her face and the unshed tears which brightened her eyes that he had frightened her, he forced himself to be calm.

"Ella, I'm sorry. I should have been with you more often, discussed our travelling plans, the luggage you can take, the things you'll need, and more importantly the things you won't need. I just thought you realized…" The exasperation returned and he breathed deeply before he continued. "Thank your parents for their generosity, the dinner service is beautiful, but try to understand, and make them understand, our life will be primitive. No dinner parties, no theatre visits, no other people for much of the time. I have all we need to cook with, to drink from, to eat off. And it *is* plain, serviceable but plain. No fancy tablecloths or napkins, no crystal goblets. Ella, you must understand, you must, we take only what we need to survive."

She had nodded and no more was said that day. But Ella had spent her evening emptying her trunks of all her treasures, in a mood of deep disquiet. She knew he had to guide her but surely he had no need to scare her. Never mind. She would respect his wishes and take only the bare essentials. He was a bachelor. He did not realize how comfortable his life could become with a woman's touch. But she would respect his wishes. All these "non essentials" would be stored here with her parents until he saw they had need of them and it was time to send for them. Or, even better, when they set up home here in Carnoustie, as surely they would do when he had the taste of Canada out of his system. In the meantime, she supposed, there would be adequate stores where they were going to furnish their house to her pleasing. Still, she would keep her cut-glass flower vases. Even wild flowers she would gather from the countryside could look elegantly displayed. Modest though her requirements were, she was anxious Sandy's friends and neighbours would know she came from a refined and distinguished family with means.

And suddenly it was all over: the wedding, the lavish luncheon party given by her parents in an enormous marquee set up in their garden, all the good wishes and the happy tears, the hugs and kisses and promises to write. At Sandy's insistence they left immediately for Glasgow by train to board the ship for Montreal, rather than spend the night nearer home. It would be tiring, he acknowledged, but it was better to make the break quickly rather than drag it out. He knew all too well the near-hysteria that could generate when the reality of a departure set in.

They were indeed exhausted when they reached their ship and were eventually installed in their cabin. Again there had been words when Sandy had seen the volume of her baggage. This time she had argued with him, declaring it all to be essential and, realizing there was now nothing that could be done about it, he had shrugged and, with an ominous "wait and see", changed the subject.

Finally they were alone, nervous with each other, each anticipating and yet dreading the night ahead. Sandy, until this moment, had given little thought to the sexual side of their marriage, seeing Ella throughout only as a sensible and pleasant companion. He was not attracted to her physically; what if he failed
to become aroused? It was inconceivable. Once he felt her
naked body warm against his there would be no problem, he
told himself and, suitably assured, he entered the bathroom so
she could undress alone.

Ella's thoughts were of an entirely different nature. Her
head filled with stories from friends and novels of men thrust-
ing themselves rampantly on unwilling females, of her mother's
warnings of blood and pain, she was almost panic-stricken in
her apprehension.

When it happened it was a disappointment to them both.
Gentle with her at first, Sandy had rapidly lost control. His
climax was quick and unsatisfactory and, angry with himself for
his insensitivity, he'd kissed her unfeelingly and turned his back
on her to sleep. Ella had enjoyed his caresses at first, surprising
herself with her lack of embarrassment and alarm when she
felt his penis harden against her. But the act itself was joyless
and painful. Even worse was his dismissal of her when he had
taken his pleasure. She felt used and unloved. Long before she
had finished cleaning herself and her nightgown, he had fallen
into a deep and noisy sleep. She looked at him with resentment
and wondered already what would become of them.

CHAPTER 15

Sandy woke the next morning, recalled immediately the fiasco of the night before and resolved to remedy his shameful performance with patience and understanding. He was still not sure whether women were supposed to find pleasure in the sexual act but he knew he could have shown her more tenderness. Tonight he would woo her. Ella was not in bed beside him but he heard noises from the bathroom. She seemed to be taking forever and, now anxious to use the facilities himself, he approached the door, was about to knock when he heard painful retching sounds from within.

Ella had woken from a restless sleep just as the dawn was breaking and, lying quietly beside her husband, she became aware of the heaving of the ship beneath her. She tried to concentrate on other matters but the persistent and uneven rocking brought on waves of nausea until she was forced into the bathroom. Now at last, with her stomach emptied, she was able, with Sandy's help, to stagger back to her bed where she prayed for an early death.

Sandy was faultless in his attentions. A good sailor himself, he was able to minister to her, sympathise with her and assure her that her misery would come to an end eventually. But day followed day and still she lay prostrate, heaving now on an empty stomach, bringing up only the water that Sandy often forced her to drink. It was not until the ship reached its destination that he was able to persuade her to climb the stairs and walk the deck, where the smell of the fresh sharp air lifted her spirits and made her feel she could face life again.

Relief was brief, however, as they transferred in Montreal from the cross-Atlantic steamer to a sturdy ice-breaker owned by the company which would take them to their final destination. Now they hugged the coastline, from the Labrador Sea into the Hudson Strait, putting in regularly to the tiny remote coastal outposts where the company had a station. Now Ella was not sick from the movement of the ship or the waves that lashed against its sides. Fog and icebergs became her terror; great mountains of ice, with peaks and turrets, white and sparkling when the sun infrequently lit upon them, with blue lights in their centres. Sandy told her that the biggest part was under the water but she found that inconceivable and, if it were true, petrifying. How, she demanded, could the boat avoid striking them with all that massive danger hidden below? With the fog rolling in daily, she determined the passage was unnavigable.

Sandy's unease grew. Ella's unreasonable panic alarmed him. He had expected a reaction from her when they entered at last the territory he regarded as his home. Yes, he had anticipated her initial shock when the first of the icebergs had appeared but once he had reassured her of their safety, of the captain's skill and knowledge of his ship and the waters he was sailing, he thought she would have relaxed and seen at last the magnificent beauty of her surroundings. Whereas he felt elation at his return to this incomparable seascape, he could sense her depression grow.

A renewal of their intimacy proved impossible. After her sickness had abated he had attempted to coax her into his arms as they lay together in their bed. But she had turned from him, excusing herself because of tiredness or weakness or headache, often feigning sleep when he knew she was awake and rigid with distaste for him. And because of the shame of his wedding night performance and concern for her recent sickness, Sandy respected her wishes.

They arrived at Port Harrison in the early morning but Sandy, excited at his return and aware of the amount of work ahead of them, was dressed and ready long before the first boat from the station nudged up against the ice-breaker. He had warned Ella that she might be neglected that day. There was the unloading to be organized, not only of their luggage but more importantly of the stores for the station that were to last them throughout the year. She had listened in silence, her mouth a thin line of displeasure. Sandy had sighed but knowing the urgency of the work and the captain's need to unload and take his ship quickly out of the area before the Hudsons Bay and Straits began to freeze for the winter, he put her out of his mind.

The work went quickly and efficiently, boats plying to and fro between the ship and the trading station. Sandy's pleasure at meeting the helpers from his station, his excitement at the prospect of running his own operation and his satisfaction at a job well done brought a huge smile to his face and in the early evening, tired but enthusiastic, he went below decks to their cabin to collect his wife.

"There are only your cabin trunks to be taken ashore now. I thought you might like to say goodbye to the captain."

She sat implacably on the bed, her hands folded tidily in her lap and, raising her eyes to his, declared, "I'm not coming."

He looked at her in astonishment and disbelief, momentarily at a loss for words. "I beg your pardon?" he managed weakly at last.

"I'm not coming. I want you to arrange for my passage back. It should be very simple. A new ticket and a telegraph to Montreal to secure my place on the steamer back to Scotland."

He sank heavily down on to the bed beside her. "I understand you've been unhappy. I can sympathise with your apprehension but we're married! You're my wife – for better or worse, I think you promised. I don't think you're giving our marriage a fair chance, Ella. Here we are, barely weeks together and sea sickness and a fear of the unknown have been your only testing grounds. Where's the woman eager for adventure and anxious to share the wilderness with me?"

He tried to touch her but she shrugged off his hand. Now her shoulders shook and the tears streamed down her cheeks as she struggled, between sobs, to justify herself.

"I've never been so unhappy in all my life," she wept. "I wish I'd died with the sea-sickness and they had thrown my body into the Atlantic. Anything rather than the ignominy of returning to Carnoustie and my parents and facing my failure."

"Then why return?" he began but she ignored his interruption and stumbled on. "How could you expect me to live in such desolation? How could you! I knew it would be primitive, you told me so, but this is an isolation impossible to imagine. I have looked at the shore and there is nothing. Only a collection of huts, one of which a sailor tells me will be my home! A cottage I was prepared for, with a garden to tend, a village to walk to. But all I see are shacks, dirty little hovels in a featureless landscape, no trees, no hills. And those men who came to help you unload. Smelly grinning savages, jibbering away in some heathen tongue which you seem to understand... oh!" She collapsed completely now and lay, her body racked with sobs, incoherent, verging on the hysterical.

And Sandy knew it was hopeless. Useless to remind her he had painted for her this very picture, or so he thought, in her living room in Carnoustie. Pointless to attempt to persuade her to reconsider, give it a try. Because she was seeing his home at its best. The weather was fair, the flowers were enjoying their brief period of bloom on the tundra. To him it was beautiful. Ahead of them were the blizzards and the whiteouts and the terrifying power of the snow and ice. Then she could be expected to regret perhaps this lonely and difficult life. It would be another year before the ship returned. He would be trapping a terrified animal, one that could possibly go insane. He would have to let her go. If there had been time for tenderness between them maybe she would have made the effort. But it had all been too quick. They barely knew each other and now he sensed she felt betrayed and misled. He touched her shoulder gently.

"It's all right, my dear. I'll make the arrangements. I'm sorry but I think I understand."

Amid surreptitious but shocked glances from all the deck

hands, he boarded the last dingy to leave the ship and, with a faint wave at the captain, Sandy turned his gaze firmly to shore. Ella had remained below decks in their cabin, all her trunks carried again below and only a few words of farewell between them. He was still numbed by the development, alternating between anger with her, despair at such a rapid failure of his marriage and an agonizing embarrassment that all this drama had taken place in full view of a shipful of men. He still had explanations to give those on shore who were eagerly awaiting the arrival of his new bride and to the company who had welcomed his marriage with a more than generous present. Should he tell feeble lies – she'd suddenly become unwell, some woman's complaint – or just blurt out the truth briefly and bluntly and have done with it? He chose the latter option, knowing his inherent lack of guile would trip him up eventually and he would stumble his way into some inconsistency. People would respect his honesty and refrain from further questions. They might discuss among themselves his bad fortune, or bad judgement, but it would be a two-day wonder and the real problems of living and working would quickly replace the gossip.

He was curiously unaffected emotionally by Ella's defection. After all, they had spent weeks closeted together in an uncomfortable but he had hoped gradual understanding of each other. He had enjoyed her company at first, especially their time together in Scotland before the wedding. Her pretty voice had charmed him and her intelligence and forthright opinions had encouraged him to overlook the obvious flaws in this doomed arrangement. He realized now that he probably would never have grown to love her, that he had been seduced by the notion of love, the appeal of a wife and children, but that even if she had chosen to face the hard life he offered her he would have regarded her more as a decent mate, a good friend, than as a lover. And later, when her sickness and unhappiness had come to the fore, he knew he had made superhuman efforts to replace with sympathy his natural annoyance and irritability at her weakness and irrational fear. Could it really be for the best that she had made this decision to return? He decided it was and acknowledged his relief at her absence without guilt.

He knew his name would be blackened back in Carnoustie when Ella returned and blamed him, as she genuinely believed, for his deceit. It would be hard on his parents too, bearing the unspoken but nonetheless hurt bewilderment which the Richardson family would be bound to display towards them. Sandy knew he had some letters to write, to attempt to explain and apologise. But he had the easy part. He was thousands of miles away from the pain and embarrassment that would manifest itself upon Ella's return. And he was heartily thankful for that. A flaw of personality maybe, but a very human failing, he thought, grinning at last with relief at his timely escape.

CHAPTER 16

From: Mrs. A. Lunan   To: Mr. A. Lunan,
Ardmore,   Revillon Freres,
Carnoustie,   Port Harrison,
Angus,   Quebec,
Scotland.   Canada.

Dated 30th March, 1925

Dear Sandy,

My return journey to Scotland was uneventful. I am happy to report that perversely I seem to have found my sea legs and in spite of inclement weather and turbulent seas across the Atlantic, I suffered no discomfort.

As expected, my arrival back in Carnoustie caused great consternation and alarm, both our families distraught at my early return. I told them that the post at Port Harrison was completely unsuitable for a white woman, that you had not appreciated the impossibility of my residing there until you saw for yourself upon our arrival the incongruity of the situation. I said we had both agreed I would return to Scotland and wait out the duration of your tenure at Port Harrison. Although this will probably be for a period of five years we had decided it was for the best and you would work towards achieving a more suitable and civilized posting for your next appointment, whereupon I would, of course, join you willingly. I have to report that all were satisfied, if not entirely happy, with this explanation. Your lack of judgement in transporting me to such an inhospitable area has been deemed unfortunate but as I appear otherwise content, my family have accepted the situation and enjoy having me home again.

I will attempt to catch the summer boat with this letter but appreciate your reply may not reach me until the following year. How strange. We *were to be closeted together for years in almost impossible interdependency had I stayed in Canada. Now we can speak only in one-sided statements, aeons of time elapsing before an old thought can be commented upon, a denial issued, an idea elaborated.*

I hope this finds you in good health and spirits.
Fondly,
Ella

* * *

Letter from:
Mr. A. Lunan,
Revillon Freres,
Port Harrison,
Quebec,
Canada.

To: Mrs. A. Lunan,
Ardmore,
Carnoustie,
Angus,
Scotland.

Dated 4th June, 1926

Dear Ella,

I am writing this in anticipation of the arrival of the "Republic" next month with the mail and next year's stores. Thank you for your letter and the back copies of "The Scotsman", which I will put in date order and read, albeit a year later, on the relevant day. It is a discipline which I find soothing. I would have replied immediately but such was the volume of goods and equipment which arrived by last year's boat that I was occupied solidly for two days unloading and the captain was anxious to leave the area, having many ports of call before the winter freeze began. This year, as you see, I am well prepared and with time on my hands before the "postman" arrives.

I note your explanation to our families of your unexpected and premature return to Scotland. I understand your reasons but regret that your parents' former regard for me has been undoubtedly damaged and my own family remain puzzled by what they term my "treatment" of you. I still, in all honesty, believe I gave you fair warning of the conditions here, of the rigours you could expect to encounter and of the harshness of the land and climate. However, whoever made the mistakes, they were made and that is an end to it. I cannot comment upon your expectation that I will be given, or even seek, a "more suitable and civilized posting" as you put it, for my next position. For the time being I like it well enough here and am pleased to report that my work has found satisfaction with the company.

Trade has gone well and our profits at the station have risen with a rich fur season and ever-increasing prices for pelts in the world market.

You will be interested to hear that our R.C.M.P. (Royal Canadian Mounted Police, in case you are unfamiliar with the initials, although I am sure you appreciate our man here, Bob Daniels, is not of the mounted variety!) has taken a wife. She is called Wilma and has taken to life here at the station like a duck to water. Of course she is second generation Canadian, from Northern Quebec, and came from solid stock, well used to deprivation and an isolated existence. She makes excellent bread on her temperamental stove and has taken to baking an extra batch which Bob kindly passes my way. She has brought a welcome and refreshing warmth to our bachelor existence. I think you would have liked her.

It is our busy time these pleasant summer months with the Inuit coming in daily to trade with the rewards of their winter hunting and trapping. Already we are seeing many fine pelts. I think we will be able to show good figures again this year.

My best wishes for your continuing good health and happiness. Please pass on my kindest regards to your family.

Your Aye,
Sandy

CHAPTER 17

Kunee lifted up the new born baby, still covered in its birthing fluids, to her husband and her son.

"I think we should call her Shawnee," she smiled. "Angus has his Scottish name, we must give his sister a Cree name. Isn't she beautiful, your little sister?" she insisted and burst into laughter as Angus wrinkled up his nose in disgust.

"You'll like her a lot better after we've cleaned her up," William reassured him. "I know you were hoping for a brother but once she grows a bit she'll be just like a boy. You can teach her everything you know about hunting and trapping. You two will make a fine team. But you have to give her time to grow!" William interjected quickly as Angus made to unsheathe his hunting knife to show the baby. "I think you'll find all she wants to do for a little while is sleep and eat. Which is what your mother should be doing now – sleeping. All that effort giving us Shawnee takes it out of her, you know. Let's take the baby, wash her down – gently! – and then pop her in the cradle to rest. You can help me." He kissed Kunee and took the tiny creature in his hands. "She's perfect, thank you darling."

William wondered that day if life could be any sweeter. He felt he had been blessed beyond belief in this life he had chosen for himself and Kunee. They had left the trapping lands of her father and the tribe and followed the trail of the fur-bearing animals which provided their livelihood. The fox, the musquash, lynx, pine marten and, on occasion, bear, were all targets but the beaver yielded their most valuable fur in this region at the southernmost end of James Bay. It was summer now and they were with others from the area, in a tented camp. After the isolation of the winter, when the main work of hunting and trapping was done, they enjoyed the company, looked forward to reunions, celebrations, feasts, marriages and of course this very special event, the birth of his daughter. William was grateful that Kunee had birthed in the summer when she had help from her sister braves. Angus too had put in an appearance at the right time of year. The summer brought a change of diet; there were migratory birds to kill and eat, their eggs a valuable source of protein for Kunee in her last weeks of pregnancy; the lake yielded a seemingly endless supply of char and trout. And with very little effort, it seemed, William had become a wealthy man. Years of harvesting the richest and glossiest of furs had brought a rich reward. Prices and demand were high, William and his family's needs were modest. He used his money only to buy ammunition and the paraphernalia his trade required.

It was too good to last.

Then came the summer of 1930. Largely cut off from the outside world from one summer to the next, William was unaware of the depression in the western world, the stockmarket crash and the drastic decline of the fur market. Few of his pelts were purchased that summer and for once he found himself worrying about the winter ahead. Kunee was, as usual, optimistic.

"They will need your furs again," she promised. "My family lived through many times of scarcity but always we survived and the next year there would be an abundance and again we would feast," she beamed.

Grateful for her serenity, William kissed her and smiled with her. But he was now troubled. Perhaps it was time to leave this nomadic existence of theirs and make their way back to civilisation. Perhaps he could even take his lovely wife and their perfect children to Scotland. Perhaps at last the rift with his family would be healed. He had dollars. Money counted for little out here. Apart from the supplies he needed to buy for their winter hunting, the notes he had been paid over the years for his furs had gone untouched. He was a moderately wealthy man. But how long would that last if the fur market stayed in decline?

There may come a time when he would be trapped himself, an ageing white man in a land cruel even to its indigenous peoples. He knew he could survive when the going was easy but what if his luck had now run out?

He began to make his plans although he kept his thoughts to himself. No need to worry Kunee until he had a formulated scheme to present to her. She was aware of his withdrawal but she knew it would pass. He was still young in the ways of the Indian. He needed to be tested, she thought stoically. And then, when they had ridden out the bad fortune and the good came again, he would be stronger for the experience.

September came and in a leisurely fashion, hunting and fishing as they went along, William and his family arrived at their winter camp. They were alone this year, their nearest neighbour some fifty miles away, but almost immediately it seemed that luck was with them. William surprised and shot a huge black bear. Plentiful in fat before its winter hibernation, it would provide them with meat and a beautiful fur for future trade or their own warmth should the winter prove harsh.

It was indeed harsh, as cold and cruel a winter as even Kunee could remember. But day after day William forced himself to leave the warmth and comfort of the tepee to check his traps and hope for a kill. They had the dried fish that Kunee had prepared in the autumn but the bear meat was now finished and they needed fresh meat to sustain them.

Unknown to his wife, William was driven by more than his need to feed his family. He was obsessed with the desire to trap silver fox. This, he reasoned with himself, would be his passport to Scotland. Rare and extremely valuable, the beautiful pelt would boost his winter income by hundreds of dollars. He could return to Carnoustie successful and wealthy, able to present his own wonderful family to those he still loved and longed to see. Even the slump in the fur market would not affect the price given for a silver fox pelt.

He made ready for a journey that would carry him beyond the usual limits of his hunting grounds, where talk had been in the summer camp of abundant sightings of the neat tracks of the white fox in the snows of the previous winter. He took little food, hoping to live off what he hunted on his way. It was important to leave Kunee and the children as much meat as he could. He would be gone, he told her, a week, maybe longer. Excited and confident of his success, he strapped on his snow-shoes and with only one backward glance, disappeared with the dog and sled into the dark snow-laden reaches of the forest.

Kunee shivered and gathered the children to her. Suddenly she was unhappy.

CHAPTER 18

The snow started on his third day out. Already he was concerned about the lack of game available to supply him with food. All of his traps were empty and a half-starved hare had provided the only fresh meat for him and the dog. Otherwise they had existed on the strips of dried fish he had brought with him.

It was gentle to begin with. Large flakes drifting slowly down to join the heavy white canopy above him. The forest was silent, the noise of any living creature in his vicinity deadened by the depth of the snow all around. William felt he was completely alone in this white wilderness. But he had hunted many times in these conditions and so he trudged on, convinced his next trap would contain his holy grail, the silver fox, or at least, he acknowledged grudgingly, a decent catch for his supper tonight.

And then the wind came. Vicious flurries which toppled the snow from the trees and whipped up the falling snow into an ecstasy of murderous attacks, the hard granules lashing into his face like ice bullets. Suddenly he was directionless. A landscape which had, minutes ago, been as familiar to him as the fields around his father's farm when he was a boy, was now featureless. All he could see when not completely blinded by the icy onslaught was white. Nothing but a white frenzy, whirling and screaming around him, a maddened ghost clutching at him enveloping him, freezing him. And the noise was terrifying. Where before there had been the silence of the frozen forest now the wailing and howling was demonic.

Panic stirred and he lunged around, staggering in circles, his hands around his eyes, his head, warding off the stinging blows of the swirling gusts and trying to protect himself from the avalanche of snow which hurled itself down from the boughs of the trees above him. In his terror he walked heavily into a tree. He fell backwards, badly winded. He gasped for air taking in mouthfuls of icy crystals, gagging, clutching at his chest in an effort to ease the stabbing pain he felt around his rib cage. But the fall had stopped the crazy pointless movement that sapped his fast-decreasing energy in a fear-driven rush to nowhere. Within seconds he was covered with a thin blanket of snow and drifts were settling heavily against him. He lay motionless, a new dread creeping into his heart. Where was the dog? More terrifying again was the realization that with the dog was his sled, his meagre provisions, his gun, his ammunition. All he had between himself and starvation was his hunting knife.

William began to call to the dog but his voice, weakened by his fall, was swallowed up and vanished in the manic wail of the wind, blotted out by the deadening volume of the snow. He stopped and, curling himself tighter into a foetal knot, he rested his head on his hands and waited for the blizzard to abate.

Kunee sat with her children inside the teepee and listened to the storm screaming its fury, battering the deerskin walls with elemental power. She was almost insane with its noise. For three days now the howling had been constant, the incessant shrieking physically painful in its intensity. She felt a dull ache inside her, a dreadful sureness of her loss. They had been protected from total immersion in the drifting snow by a windbreak that William had fashioned around the teepee at the first indication of the severity of this winter. They were now marooned in an island banked about by ten-foot walls of snow, the branches of the windbreak straining under the burden of their weight. Kunee knew another day of unrelenting storm would cause their protection to collapse and they would be smothered by the falling walls, crushed under the avalanche.

But as suddenly as it had started the blizzard faltered and then stopped. Kunee allowed herself to hope once again.

William had been gone a week, he had anticipated the length of this trip, she told herself, and he had warned her. But he had never been out in a storm like the one she had just survived. He would have built himself a shelter, she reasoned, and sat out the storm just as she and the children had done. He would have meat from his traps to feed himself, he would boil snow on his primus stove to make water, and even if he was unable to cut wood or gather brush to make a fire he and the dog would huddle together to keep warm. Even now he would be making his way back to her, crazy with worry for her safety. In a day or two he would have returned, kissed them all, fussed over them and she would make a feast from the game he would bring home and they would lie together, bloated, happy and content to be together again. The nightmare would have ended.

The sun was shining on the eighth day of his absence and already the snow was softening, melting, no longer a fatal threat to them but now a thing of beauty as it sparkled and glistened in the light. The children were playing, pounding each other with handfuls of icy powder, rolling like two little snowballs, giggling and laughing, their relief at being out of the teepee at last as strong as Kunee's.

Suddenly there was a faint cry, a whimper only, and to their horror Scotty, William's husky dog, limped, almost dead, into their clearing. He was still pulling the sled behind him although he was tethered to it now by only one of the leather traces; the others he had bitten through and presumably eaten. Nothing remained tied to the sled and it trailed behind him awkwardly, catching at every bump as the poor creature dragged himself to Kunee and then collapsed at her feet, his tail wagging feebly.

The children did not understand. They petted and fondled the dog, rushing to get him water and food at their mother's bidding, pleased to see their friend again. But Kunee's heart was breaking and her eyes spilled hot tears of grief and despair. William was dead. There was now no doubt in her mind. He could not have survived without the dog and the provisions on the sled. There was no fear for herself and her children in her misery. She knew that soon others would come looking for them, knowing the family to be alone this year in their winter camp. A blizzard of such ferocity would have caused their neighbours to think of them and they would not rest until some-one had checked that they were safe. William would have done the same.

Oh William! Her whole being ached and she dared not think of life without him. Her strength would grow slowly, but it would grow. The children needed her. But now, with her pain raw and new, she allowed herself an outpouring of her grief. She wailed to the heavens in anguish, sobbing out her hurt and despair. The children clustered to her, frightened by her distress and they too cried with her, mercifully unaware of their loss.

CHAPTER   19

"You've done a grand job here, Sandy!" enthused Mick Stewart. "We'll be sorry to see you go but one man's loss is another man's gain, so they say, and the powers that be in Montreal want you back there to discuss a new assignment. I've a notion of where it is but," he winked and tapped the side of his nose with a knowing gesture, "least said soonest mended."

Sandy grinned weakly. Least said in your case, he thought. A few hours of Mike's friendly but completely cliché-ridden conversation had left him eager to be off. Mike was replacing him and Sandy pitied the young apprentice clerk who would be assigned to the post with him. Two years listening to these inanities meant a prospective suicide here, he reflected darkly.

The visit to Montreal and the Canadian headquarters of the company left him in a state of shock and euphoria. Convinced he would be moved to somewhere safe and civilized, especially as he knew rumours of his wife's unacceptance of hardship had reached the higher echelons, he was stunned when a map of the Northern Territories was spread out before him and there, at approximately the geographic centre of Canada, two degrees south of the Arctic circle, was Baker Lake. They wanted him there. Baker Lake, in the province of Keewantin, the North Wind, the heart of the Barrenlands. The names alone thrilled Sandy and he knew without hesitation that this was where he wanted to be. He was due leave, six months, and a trip to Scotland had been scheduled. But how could he go and face the cries of shock and horror from his own family, the silent accusatory stares of Ella and her family; Ella, who expected him to beg for comfort and civilization and in return would bestow her presence and favours upon him? No. He would keep his distance, spend his time in Montreal, perhaps take a trip to Toronto or to Prince Edward Island to see Aggie and Bill, and then a leisurely journey on the company boat up the western coast of the Hudson Bay to his new home.

He arrived, two months early, in the August of 1929. It was cold, the promise of an early snowfall in the air but the cold was a blessing, killing the mosquitos and black fly that plagued the area in the milder months of June and July. The tundra was aglow with its summer flowers; the tall lichens, pale gray and dull green, matting with alpine heather, blueberry, pink bearberry and a sprinkling of ferns. The tiny leaves of the miniature shrubs bright green and orange; in some places purple splashes of Arctic foreweed, the yellow of Arctic poppy and arnica; in the gullies by the side of the lake, aged willows two feet high, gnarled and twisted like bonsai trees. Sandy was enchanted.

He was met by the out-going manager, Tam McTaggert, a bluff Scot of few words, who showed him to the station manager's house and left him with abrupt apologies to his own devices as he and the station clerk began the frantic work of unloading the year's stores from the boat. Aware of the urgency from his time at Port Harrison, Sandy offered to help.

"Make the most of the rest, Mr. Lunan," advised McTaggart, "you'll have plenty to do on the morrow when I'm away and the boxes have to be moved from the beach to the warehouses. There's snow on the way and you'll have to get the freight stowed before the dried goods get wet and ruined. A year without your supply of flour and sugar and oats would be a bad start," he remarked with gloomy satisfaction.

Stung by the implication that he had a lot to learn about life in the Arctic, Sandy was about to fling a terse rejoinder to McTaggart's retreating back but then he smiled. The man was right. Sandy had experienced ship-time since his first year with the company and he knew the routine blindfolded. But it was worth reminding a man of his continual battle with the elements and of being prepared at all times.

He wandered outside to watch the frenzy of activity on the shoreline. The sun was shining, bathing the settlement in a silver sheen. The reflection on the calm waters of the lake frosted the ship with sparkling flecks of brightness. Lighting up a cigarette, Sandy settled himself on a bale of flour and breathed deeply.

McTaggart left with the final barge in the morning and as the foghorn of the departing supply ship sounded Sandy called his young clerk Norman and together they went towards a room at the front of the house, where Norman had told him the Inuit were usually received by the station manager.

"They'll be keen to meet you, sir," he enthused. "Normally they would have gone now the summer trading is over but most of the families decided to stay on to greet you. They're a friendly bunch."

There was a babble of noise from inside and when Sandy pushed open the door he was faced with a room overflowing with beaming faces. Women and children sat flat-legged on the floor, crowded against the people around them. One woman was nursing a baby at her breast. The men were packed on the bench alongside the table; others perched on the table itself, while the rest stood against the wall. Everyone was talking and laughing. A smell of unwashed bodies hung in the air. And still smiling and giggling amongst themselves, they pushed forward to shake his hand. No firm grip to denote masculine strength, no pumping of each other's hand, just a light clasp by each Inuik man, woman and child, the hand raised to eye level before being released. They spoke their names and chuckled encouragingly as he repeated the unfamiliar sounds and syllables, attempting to commit, with no success, each one to memory. He spoke Inuktitut but it was a different dialect from the language they used here and he knew it would take time to learn their speech and their ways. No matter. Time he had in plenty and already he was warming to these happy people. It would be no hardship to become their friend.

He knew he would have to relearn much of what he had assimilated at Port Harrison. There he had dealt with the coastal

Inuit, a people who existed on a varied diet of walrus, porpoise, Arctic hares, Arctic char, ptarmigan and, on occasion, polar bear. But their mainstay was the seal. A creature which supplied them with food, clothing, shelter, heat, light and transportation. Their existence was uncertain, desperate hunger often their lot with the vagaries of the weather and the unreliability of a hunting season.

But these people he was now amongst had, before the advent of the white man with his trading demands, only one target. The caribou. And so they were called "the people of the deer". Limited to this single food staple, the inland Inuit were totally dependent upon the caribou migrations. A hunting group could be camped in the usual migratory path of the deer but if, for some reason, they veered only a slight distance from their route, the hunters would miss them completely and starvation was a very real possibility. Now they hunted also the white fox and bartered these furs with the white trading companies for food and ammunition. But the caribou was still their primary and natural game. Sandy knew it must stay that way. Anxious though he was to carry out his duties for his company as conscientiously and successfully as he was able and to secure a steady profit for his own station, he respected and admired the age-old tradition of these inland hunters. Already he was instinctively aware that their dependence on the white man's food was a mistake. Under his regime, he resolved grimly, the people of the deer would keep their name.

It was a busy day that first day he spent in his new home. Dragging cases and boxes and bales of merchandise from the beach to the warehouses, Sandy, Norman and a host of eager Inuit helpers turned the beach in front of the post into a trampled mass of slush and sand as the first flakes of snow drifted lazily down from the sky. Soon everything was blanketed under a soft white layer. They worked well into the evening darkness by the light of gas lanterns but at last all the precious stores were safe from the damp in the warehouses. Sandy surveyed their work with satisfaction.

"Time for a tot of rum." He patted the young clerk on the back. "We've deserved it."

CHAPTER 20

He spent the following week making the acquaintance of the few other white men who lived around the sixty mile length of Baker Lake. In a community as small and as isolated as this, it was essential that they know each other, a bonus if they liked each other. Sandy was fortunate in this case. He realized quickly and with relief that here the company was congenial and he could not have wished for better if he had chosen them himself. There were his rivals at the Hudsons Bay company at the west side of the lake, Archie Hunter and his assistant Bill Hislop. There were the two RCMP representatives Corporal 'Nick' Nichols and Constable Herb Humphries. Finally there were the two missionaries, the Reverend Jimmy James representing the Anglican faith and the dark-bearded Father Rio, an Oblate priest of the Catholic mission. From these last two Sandy kept at a comparative distance although the Father he found to be a mild and inoffensive man of the cloth, not too overbearing in his missionary zeal.

Throughout his time with the Inuit people, Sandy had regarded the Christian missions with profound irritation. Why, he reasoned on numerous occasions, burden an essentially moral people with the trappings of a Western-based religion which, in effect, refused to translate to their unique lifestyle? The Inuit lived by all the right standards. They were kind, loving and honest. Their innate goodness needed no bolstering or changing by proselytising zealots. There were excellent men amongst those Christian brothers, Sandy admitted freely, but ignore their message he implored silently, keep to your own immeasurably superior tenets that have served you well in this forbidding land. By all means welcome the singer but do not listen to his song.

And in the case of the Reverend James, Sandy concluded, you will be forgiven if you do not make the effort at all.

He found it easy to bond with this minuscule community. He was instantly popular when they discovered he was a ham radio enthusiast and operator, opening up their necessarily isolated existence to contact with the outside world. Within days they were unable to imagine how they had existed without this wonderful connection, although the novelty wore off equally quickly and instead of a diverting form of entertainment, it remained a reassuring tool in times of emergency.

It took a near disaster to alert them all as to how useful his radio could be. Stomach heavy with the rich remains of a caribou stew he and Norman had shared with the two men from the HBC post, Sandy woke in the pre-dawn and for what seemed an eternity tossed and turned, unable to go back to sleep, his mind full of irrelevancies, his body a mass of discomfort. The wind howled outside, a blizzard which had whipped itself into being shortly after the visitors had left. Suddenly there was a thud as the door of the house bulleted open, and into the hall, blue with cold and exhaustion, staggered Archie and Bill. Sandy and Norman wasted no time with questions until after the two men had been thawed, divested of their parkas and, sitting beside the newly-stoked fire with steaming mugs of tea warming their hands, were obviously on the road to recovery.

"You probably didn't expect to see us back so soon," began Archie shamefacedly, "but stew like that, well it's hard to stay away from. We were hoping for second helpings," he quipped weakly.

"Come on, man! Out with it. You've obviously had a fright. Less of the bullshit, let's have the story!" barked Sandy and then, relenting, added gently, "Second helpings, you'll be lucky. Norman here polished off the lot only minutes after you left."

"We were O.K. until the wind got up. We ran into Peter, you know, one of Nick's Inuit. He'd been to see Father Rio at the mission and he told us not to cross the lake but to follow the shoreline back home. By then it was blowing heavens hard and we knew it would take us longer to walk round so we ignored his advice, put our heads down and struggled out over the ice." Bill Hislop's fair complexion, which had been a frightening ghostly white only minutes earlier, was at last reviving and a pink flush now coloured his cheeks.

His boss continued the story. "In no time at all the landmarks had disappeared in the drifting snow and the wind, swirling round, had edged us further and further onto the lake without our knowing. We knew we should have reached the HBC post after about fifteen minutes but allowing for the heavy going and the fact that we were walking into a wind, we didn't start worrying until we'd been ploughing on well over half an hour and still hadn't reached home. I said to Bill then we'd obviously been going in the wrong direction so we turned round and walked with the wind, hoping we'd reach shore and some recognizable landmark."

They looked at each other, recalling vividly the nightmare of the last few hours and Archie continued: "After another hour we knew we were well and truly lost and the best thing we could do would be to sit it out. We hollowed out a hole in a deep snow drift to shelter in. You can guess the rest. We both fell asleep."

"My God!" muttered Sandy. "That could have been the end of you."

"I know. But something woke Bill and he found we were snowed in. We were completely covered up, could hardly move, it had drifted right over us. You'd probably not have found us until the thaw." Archie gulped another mouthful of his tea. "We dug ourselves out and from then on until the first signs of daylight we took it in turns running up and down the ridge for five or ten minutes. As soon as we could see we set out again, made our way back to the lake ice that we'd obviously left without knowing it and found our way back to you. I tell you, Sandy, I've never been so pleased to see anyone before!"

The tension relieved, they all made fatuous jokes about the indigestibility of the stew which had obviously woken Bill and saved their lives but their near brush with death was a sobering thought. Sandy came to a decision.

"Of course you were fools to venture anywhere without your snow knives. Had either of you had his you could have built a proper shelter instead of that snow hole that nearly served as your grave. But I'll tell you what else we'll do. I'll string a telegraph line between the Revillon post, the HBC station and the RCMP's place and I'll teach you Morse Code. From now on, anyone who doesn't report in within half an hour of leaving any of the stations will be regarded as missing and a search party will be dispatched. It might result in a whole pile of false alarms but you can never be too careful and I've always found the more insurance you have, the less chance you have of needing it."

CHAPTER 21

The time of the great starvation was the year Akumalik became a wife and mother. She was only twelve years old. Her childhood had been sweet before that time. Howmik and Ootek, her mother and father, Kala her sister and Aljut her brother lived with the members of two other families, a simple but happy existence, basking in the love and warmth that is every Inuit child's birthright. In the camps of the People the child is king. "While you are young, while life is easy, find what joys you may," Howmik told her children, "for childhood is short and tragedy often follows."

And so Akumalik played. But as she played she learned. She tended the fires under the cooking pot, sometimes far into the night when the adults were asleep, and no one scolded her telling her she must sleep. When she was tired she slept, when she was hungry she ate. No strict regime ordered her young life for as she played she watched and learned and imitated, knowing soon without chastisement or punishment her role in this family and her place in the camp.

They lived the life of the People. They hunted Tuktu, the deer. In the springtime, when the does' bellies hung heavy with fawn, the hunters came out of their tents and saw that the kayaks were ready. While the women and children shouted and clapped their hands at the passing herds of deer, frightening them down to the banks of the river, the hunters launched their kayaks and the spring killing began. Spears flashed in the sun and dead deer floated down with the current into the bays below. The fresh meat was welcome after the frozen flesh that had been their diet all winter. And in the autumn Tuktu came again, fleeing south before the approach of winter. Now their fur was rich and thick, the fine hides perfect for clothing and bedding. The meat was cut and cured, cached ready for the long months ahead when the caribou had gone.

But in 1926 Tuktu did not come. For generations her family had waited for the deer at the ancestral hunting grounds and for decades the deer had come to them in their tens of thousands. But day followed day that autumn and the hunters waited in vain. Then the snows began and Ootek knew they should leave. They would have to search for Tuktu elsewhere and, failing that, he would have to kill the Arctic hare, the ptarmigan, no substitute for the rich bounty provided by the caribou, but food at least for his family.

And so the famine approached. Now in their winter igloos the three families began to starve. Although the men were fine hunters, there was no food to be found. Nothing seemed to crawl or creep or bound in the vast white emptiness. Every day they trekked from the camp, still hopeful and determined but empty-handed and full of fear as they returned.

Howmik was the first to die and she chose her own going. One night, while the rest of the family lay uneasily asleep she dragged her bony limbs from the caribou skin blanket, stripped off her clothes and crawled out through the entrance tunnel into the whining darkness of the night. For many days she had refused her own minute portion of the family food so that her children might have a little more. Now she crawled naked out of the shelter and walked into the white wind until she could walk no further. In a little while she sank to her knees and the snow rose over her. There was one less mouth to feed in Akumalik's home.

A few days later death came to her brother and sister. Younger than her and not so strong, they missed their mother sorely and their will to live vanished with her. Ootek made his decision. Now at last convinced that no winter deer would come within their reach, he had to find help. Taking Akomalik and a single skinny Arctic hare, he entered the igloo of Hekwaw. "I leave her with you," he stated. "I shall go to the trading place and in a little while I will return with food for you all." He looked beyond Hekwaw and saw to his horror the crouched form of Kooyak, lifeless on the sleeping ledge, her tiny baby frozen at her breast. Her almost naked body was bloated with starvation, the belly grotesquely distended. Hekwaw followed his eyes and nodded and with barely the strength to raise his arms, beckoned for Akumalik to join him and Nilak, his year-old son. Unwilling to leave her father, she clung to Ootek but he pushed her towards the younger man. "Do what you can till I return." He visited first the final igloo but there only silence and death greeted him. Turning his face to the north, he staggered into the frenetic fury of the wind.

It was three more days before the white men with their sleds and dogs and food found Akumalik, Hekwaw and Nilak. They sat, the young girl and the man with his baby son, huddled together for warmth, their skeletal bodies shrunken beneath the mangled hides of the caribou skins that they had chewed in vain for sustenance, their eyes bright with the onset of death. And the men fed them and comforted them and guided them to their sleds and warmth and safety. They covered up the bodies of those already dead and added to that number the lifeless body of Ootek. They had found him only yards away from their station, on his knees, crawling with his last ounce of strength to find help for his daughter. It was too late for him, he had driven himself beyond salvation but he was able, with his dying breath, to direct them to those he had left behind.

And so it happened that Hekwaw took Akumalik for his wife, bound together as they were with the harrowing memories of their tragedy and their need for a family. Akumalik had looked into the face of death and survived. Her body now a woman's, she gave birth to their daughter Martee, who she loved with a fierceness born of the loss of family and her need to create another. She took Nilak as her own. Willingly she forfeited her innocence and the carefree days of her childhood, and with Hekwaw and Nilak became another family. But this time her husband told her, they would not be a people of the deer. Instead he would hunt the fox for the white man. He would lay his traps and he would trade with those who had saved them. No longer would their lives depend upon the vagaries of the caribou, on their migratory routes. They would live near the white man. They would take from him his guns and ammunition, his flour and tea and lard and in return he, Hekwaw, would find the foxes to pay for all these goods. They would have security. Never again, he told Akumalik, would they face starvation.

CHAPTER 22

After Martee, Akumalik had no more children. It was a bitter disappointment to her and Hekwaw for they craved a large family. But she had been weak when she conceived her daughter, sickly throughout her pregnancy and the birth had been difficult. The shaman told them that the spirits did not wish them to have another child and eventually, reluctantly, they accepted his pronouncement. They joined the camp of Hekwaw's kin, two cousins, their wives and their families and again life was good. There were babies and children in their camp and Akumalik loved them all. It was compensation for her own restricted family.

Now more of the People, frightened by the great famine, had begun to work for the white man, trapping the foxes he desired so much. Tuktu came back to their lands and their old migratory routes but the people of Akumalik's camp no longer depended on the animals' return. They hunted him still for his skin was essential for their clothing and shelter, but his flesh, although welcome, was not primary to their survival. Now the white man was their security, with his guns and ammunition and the foreign foods he traded with them.

Akumalik had grown skilled with her needle and the clothes she made from the skin of the deer were prized by those for whom she sewed. First she would take the stiff untreated skin and work it between her hands until it grew soft and supple. Then she cut out her patterns. She used the skins taken from the September deer, before their coarse winter hair growth had set in, for the inner shirt which was worn hair-in to the skin. With delicate needles carved and filed from the shoulder blades of the deer, she made stitches so fine they could not be counted with the human eye. Then she took the heavier skin of the October deer and fashioned it into the outer garment, the parka, which was worn with the hair out. Stockings she made from the delicate soft skin of the fawns and footwear from the adult hides, worn hair inside and soled with the forehead patch of the animal. Pants, worn hair-in, reached only to the knee and were flared to permit free movement and air circulation to prevent sweating. Dampness and subsequent chilling could prove fatal.

She was eighteen when Hekwaw returned one day to their tent. He was laden with goods from the trading post of the white man, his supplies for the winter ahead.

"Aupaluktuk wishes a winter outfit," he informed his wife. "I said you would sew it for him." Akumalik looked up with alarm.

"I have sewn only for those I know," she protested. "Who is this man, the Red One? Where is his wife? Surely she should make his clothing."

"I have told you of him before," Hekwaw answered patiently. "He is the white man who takes my skins. I like him, he is fair. He brought this name, the Red One, from another place, but it is good. He has cheeks always red, not only when the cold makes them so. You will come with me tomorrow and measure him for the outfit. There is no wife and he had taken no woman of the People to comfort and clothe and cook for him. I told him of your skill and he inspected my clothing and said it was good. We will get more ammunition for the gun for your work."

But Akumalik was reluctant to visit the place of the white man. In vain Hekwaw alternatively coaxed and threatened. It was an inexplicable disinclination that held her back. Perhaps her memories of her brush with death when only the timely arrival of the white man saved her. But surely this should serve to make her think of his people with gratitude and pleasure? There was no reason but such was her unease and obstinacy that her husband, frustrated and perplexed, eventually gave up his attempt to persuade her.

"I cannot understand you," he concluded feebly, "and I do not know what I will tell the Red One tomorrow." He stood, thwarted and pouting, his face a comic picture of misery. At that Akomalik laughed.

"Oh I will make his clothing, and I will make it well. But there is no need for me to see the man. I will teach you how to measure him and you will bring me all the things I need to know." She brought out a length of fine sinew, taken from the broad back of the caribou and tied it around his head, across the forehead. Then she knotted it.

"This will give me his height," she pronounced. "It is always three times the circle of his head. Then you will measure his waist and knot it so, his arms, the length of his legs." At each measuring she looped the thread until along its length she had a series of knots. "And here," she flourished her measure at him, "I have all I need. Within two weeks he will have his winter furs."

And so it was done. Akumalik sewed for the white man a suit of warmth and durability and beauty. She put a fringe on the front of his parka and on the long tail flap that came down to the back of his knees. She decorated the back of the jacket with insets made from the white belly fur of the deer that contrasted with the dark fur in graceful blending. She made him mitts from the tough fur of the leg hide with the fur facing out so that the normal heat of the hand kept the hide supple and warm.

While she sewed she thought of the man who would wear these clothes. A man, her husband told her, who was trusted and admired by the People. A man who spoke their language and respected their customs. She wondered why he had chosen to live amongst them, why he had no woman of his own. And she was happy when Hekwaw told her he was pleased with his outfit, had given them a generous trading for her work and had requested Hekwaw to bring her to the station so he could thank her personally. She would not go. There was still something that troubled her and made her keep her distance from *Kabluna*, Eyebrow, as they called all white men. And so Hekwaw brought her the present, the beautiful necklace fashioned from the teeth of the walrus which he, the Red One, had brought from another place and wanted her to have along with his gratitude.

Akumalik was enchanted. She put on the ornament and pressed it to her skin, feeling the satin smoothness of the bone against her neck. She had never seen anything as lovely, nor had she ever been given anything for herself alone. The Inuit have little need nor desire for personal possessions and yet she treasured this gift and as a woman instinctively recognized its elegance. This man, the Red One, was indeed someone special, she mused. She had never met him and yet he had taken a singular place in her thoughts, he was a persistent impetus to her imagination. She caught her husband watching her curiously and quickly she stopped fingering the necklace. She picked up six-year-old Martee and cuddled her.

"Come my sweet one," she crooned, "I will show you a new string-figure, a cat's cradle, and we will play till you too can make the wolverines fight in the string."

CHAPTER 23

It was early on a June morning when the miracle occurred. Sandy was sitting at his breakfast and enjoying the last few spoonfuls of his special oatmeal, a dish so glutinous that the spoon was almost able to stand upright on its own in the mixture. He had his own supply, brought in yearly at ship-time and the steeping of the oatmeal at night ready for its slow simmer to perfection the following morning was a ritual recognized and respected quickly by Norman and any who came to visit. It was unwise to disturb or attempt even to converse with Sandy before the eating of the porridge.

Outside the rain was drumming a relentless violent tattoo on the roof of the house. And then a new sound insinuated itself into his consciousness. A sound that rivalled the muffled thunder of the rain. There was a murmur that became a roar and the house shook and the breakfast dishes slid and rattled on the table and Sandy sat for a moment, numb with fear, convinced he was experiencing his first earthquake. Recovering himself, he ran to the window where he was joined by a dishevelled Norman still wiping sleep from his terrified eyes. They watched in numbed disbelief one of nature's stunning displays of power.

The ice had not yet gone from out of the nearby Thelon river and although open water rimmed Baker Lake, a lid of partially thawed ice still covered the main part of its surface. Now the river ice had broken up and was being driven towards the lake by the water torrent produced by the springtime run off. But the jumbled mass of ice chunks and rafting flows in the river were being blocked by the sheet ice on the lake. The noise was that of grinding ice. Prevented from flowing into the lake by a dam made of its own fracturing ice, the river was building up an enormous head of water pressure. Something had to give. Before their stupefied gaze and with a thunderous roar the stupendous force of the backed-up river propelled the wall of ice out into the lake. Such was the momentum that twenty-foot walls of ice rubble piled up on the shores of the lake. Dogs chained near the lake edge disappeared under an avalanche of ice. Sleighs, boats, kayaks, anything that was in its path was swallowed up and totally destroyed. Gullies were dug in the beach and huge boulders gouged out of the earth. The devastation was immense. And in the midst of this desolation, pincered by impressive walls of ice on either side, stood the Anglican mission, untouched by this deadly flow, serene in its frail stability.

The eight members of the Baker Lake community, joined by chattering groups of visiting Inuit, surveyed the ravaged landscape and agreed with the Reverend James that a miracle had indeed taken place. Personally Sandy put it down to good luck but he was unwilling to dampen the minister's excitement and he was still impressed enough by the forces of nature to agree, half-heartedly, to an act of God. Rarely had he seen the Reverend in such good humour and that alone was a God-given gift. They dispersed eventually to their respective employments and each marvelled privately at the surprises that this Barrenland, of supposedly featureless landscape, could fling at them.

There was a surprise of a very different nature in store for Sandy that same evening. He had shared his supper with the two policemen, Nick and Herb, and now, with their hot rum toddies and their cigarettes they settled comfortably round Sandy's radio as he switched on the set and waited for it to warm up and receive messages from the outside world. Although the other two were now only mildly entertained by this link with civilization, Sandy still found it compelling and it was rare that he missed an evening's listening. The set crackled into life and the three men listened with interest as messages were received back and forth between the limited users of the radio transmission. Their interest increased when over the airwaves the staccato voice of the RCMP station manager at Churchill filled the room.

"I need to talk to Sandy Lunan, station manager of Revillion Freres, Baker Lake." The urgency of his tone was obvious in spite of the distortion of the transmission and the men leaned forward, now focused completely on the radio. Sandy announced his presence, his face grim with concentration and an unexplained foreboding.

"I think I have some bad news, Mr. Lunan," the policeman warned. "The body of a William Lunan was brought into our James Bay station this morning. A Cree Indian woman said he was her husband. There are two half-breed children, a boy and a girl. It's an unusual surname. Someone thought of you, said maybe you were related? I hope not for your sake, but could you confirm either way."

Sandy swallowed once and then, with impressive control, impassively acknowledged the relationship. "I'll be down there as soon as I can arrange transport," he concluded. "Try to encourage the family to wait for me. I should like to meet them."

Nick and Herb, shocked and silent until now, both began to speak, to offer their sympathy and support but Sandy cut them short.

"Thank you, boys. I know you mean well but you'll understand this is something I have to come to terms with. I need to be alone just now. I'll be grateful of your company eventually, when all this has sunk in, when I have made some sense of it myself, but..." He turned and walked from the room.

"I think we ought to tell the minister," ventured Nick as they made their way back to their own post. "I know he said he needed to be alone but he could probably use some comfort from the church."

"Sandy's not one for religion you know," warned Herb. "He never goes to the services. But you're right. We'd better tell Jimmy James and let him decide what should be done."

And so the Reverend James, his heart still full of the miracle of the morning, presented himself to a white-faced and taciturn Sandy. With supreme insensitivity he failed to gauge the desperate sorrow in the man as Sandy, unfailing as ever in his politeness, brewed them both a mug of tea and listened with tight-lipped control to the meaningless patter which spilled effortlessly and sanctimoniously from the minister's mouth.

"And Mr. Lunan," he summarised with practised fluency, "who are we to question God's ways? The Lord giveth and the Lord taketh away. You have lost your brother. That is indeed a terrible sadness. But only this morning you witnessed His greatness as in His infinite mercy, before your very eyes, He spared the Anglican mission!"

Sandy looked at this man of God and marvelled.

"Thank you for your visit Reverend James. Forgive me but I cannot bring myself to express the emotion that your words have aroused in me. But rest assured, I will never forget your message. And now it is late and I wish you goodnight."

Satisfied and with a humble awareness of a job well done, the minister returned to his church.

CHAPTER   24

FROM: *Mr. A. Lunan*   *To: The Lunan Family,*
Revillon Freres,   *Philip Street,*
Baker Lake,   *Carnoustie,*
Nelson River District,   *Angus*
N.W.T. Canada.   *Scotland.*

October 1931

Dear All,

You already know the dreadful news of William, but the telegram system being restricted as it is, your information would have been brief and therefore undoubtedly brutal. I know how you feel. It was the same with me when I first heard the news via my radio set. One moment I had no idea of William's whereabouts, his history since he left us in Scotland other than that he was somewhere in Canada, and in the next moment I hear he has a wife and family and has perished in the most tragic of circumstances. The shock to us all has been almost unsupportable.

But I am now comforted and I wish to share my solace with you. I visited the James Bay area as soon as I was able and arranged a decent burial and funeral for him. I am sure it would have had your approval. I have provided for the carving of a tombstone for his grave with an appropriate message from us all. He will rest peacefully in the pretty Christian churchyard in a country he had grown to love as I do.

I was delighted to find that Kunee, his wife, and their two children, Angus and Shawnee, had waited for me and were happy to meet and talk with a member of William's family. Mother, she is lovely. In every way. She is a beauty, of that there is no doubt, but her loveliness comes also from within. I am a poor hand at describing these things, and my time with her was, of necessity, brief but I feel she has a sweetness in her nature that I have rarely encountered before, especially in one so young. She has almost a spiritual serenity about her and has accepted her loss with impressive dignity. She loved William and, I am sure, had made his life a happy one. You will be moved to know that he had told her of the circumstances of his leaving Scotland and although he spoke of his initial hurt at our betrayal of him he had grown to understand our mistake and still had a deep love and longing for us, his Scottish family. We know now what a grievous wrong we did him, the girl herself admitted her duplicity after the birth of her child, so it is a supreme consolation to me to hear that he had forgiven us.

The two children are charming, bright and beautiful. The boy Angus is a miniature William, the girl, still a baby, is adorable. I enclose photographs of all three. I was anxious to know, as I know you must be also, what Kunee felt their future to be. She impressed me again with the intelligence she has shown in this matter and the thought she has given to it before reaching her decision. While the children are young she is happy to rejoin her family in their traditional camps, moving with them to their summer and winter dwelling places. She wants them to have a deep appreciation of her native heritage and to learn the many skills such a life would teach them. But William had left money. He did well as a fur trapper and trader – an irony, is it not, that we both chose, independently, a similar lifestyle? She is determined that William's children will have the benefits of his culture and race and she knows a Western education is their passport to a richer fuller life than the one she has led so far. There are many small but expanding towns springing up in the area. When the time is ripe she will take her children to their schools to give them an opportunity to learn and eventually to make their own reasoned and informed choice for their future. A singular and impressively unselfish young lady, would you not agree?

As you know I am due for leave next year and I had intended to visit Scotland and you all. But, upon reflection, I think it may be better if I plan to spend a longer period of time than I have been able to do so far, with Kunee and the children so she has a true sense of our kinship and of all the family's concern and regard for her. We owe it to William to care for her and to show our interest and it will be a small sacrifice on my part to be our representative in this matter. You will know that relations between Ella and I have deteriorated and I hear from her rarely. She is unable to accept the fact that my job is in the Arctic, that I am temperamentally unsuited to a position in Head Office in Montreal, and, even more to the point, that I do not wish such a position even if it were available. We must, therefore, live apart as she is equally reluctant to agree to any compromise. It is a sad situation to which I have no answer. Perhaps time will show us a way. Therefore, although I would dearly love to see you all, I think my decision to delay my return is, for everyone, the most sensible.

The effects of the Depression have at last reached us here and have affected us quite severely. Prime white fox pelts which we used to value at about forty dollars have now dropped to two or three dollars apiece. It is hard, indeed almost impossible, for the Inuit to understand and I am reluctant to see them suffer now they have come to depend upon the white man, instead of the caribou, for their livelihood. I have cut my own budget to the bone, as have the Hudson Bay men and the Mounties. Food and fuel supplies are limited, this year's ship-time bringing half the bounty we have come to expect. Winter has arrived early this year also and promises to be a cruel one. I have no heat at all in the house, fuel conservation is essential for what we may have to endure later. Water freezes in the glass and we wear our outside travelling clothing inside. But we survive and mostly happily. The Mounties still have their 'extras' in the food line – jam, canned fruit, bacon – so we trade with them for the extra tea and hardtack we can spare and it works out agreeable to us all. We have made it clear to our respective headquarters that visitors will be unwelcome and in fact unsustainable, until rations have been fully restored!

I see with alarm that I have covered pages in this letter, probably twice your usual allotment, and no doubt with double the quantity of mistakes in the spelling and grammar department. But I knew you would be anxious and eager to hear of my news about William and his family. I hope you join me in gaining comfort from the knowledge that, short though his life was, it was a useful and happy one and his legacy to us, in the form of his children, is rich.

I trust you are all well and prospering. I think of you daily and send you, as always, my love.

Yours Aye
Sandy

CHAPTER   25

The market in fur trading continued to plummet until the policy of operating two trading posts, Revillon Freres and the Hudson's Bay Company, at Baker Lake became no longer feasible. Since 1926 the British company had owned 51% of the French business, but had operated a system whereby both posts remained open and cooperation rather than competition aided both companies, while discouraging any independent new traders. However, by 1936 consolidation was deemed essential and Sandy was chosen to be the new post manager for the Hudsons Bay Company at Baker Lake. It was he who decided that although the Revillon site was by far the better location, the HBC building was superior and he would have that as his new home.

They chose a fine clear day in the winter to dismantle the building, stacking each partition carefully on to the sleds and guiding the dogs across the frozen lake to the site of the Revillon building. Everyone helped although, being the trapping season, there were few Inuit at the station. Ohoto, his resident store man, chuckled with Sandy as they envisaged the look of astonishment on the faces of the returning Inuit when they came to trade at the old HBC post in the spring.

"They will look and look and it will be no longer there." Ohoto found the mental picture irresistible. "And then we will wave from across the lake, they will see the company flag flying and they will think the ghosts have stolen their minds." Throughout the four days it took them to resurrect the HBC house on its new site, Ohoto broke down periodically into fresh gales of laughter as he indulged himself in his fantasy.

It was a modest structure. A living room, two bedrooms, the kitchen and an Eskimo room, the large porch where the

Inuit came to take tea and socialize. An indoor privy was added although Sandy anticipated it would be used only by the occasional female visitor to the post. He had been relieved to have had this facility available at Revillon Freres on that momentous occasion when Mr. and Mrs. Charles Lindbergh had stayed with him for two days on their historic survey flight from New York to the Orient. It had been an unnerving visit. Awed by their celebrity, he had wondered how to entertain such luminaries but, apart from attending a lunch he had hosted for the entire population of Baker Lake, they had spent most of their time refuelling and checking over their airplane. Sandy's abiding memory of his guests, the charming Mrs. Lindbergh and her surprisingly brusque husband, was of a conversation he overheard between them.

"Anne, I want the pliers."

"Which pliers, dear?"

"The only damn pliers there are!"

His life continued as it had with Revillon in the orderly passing of the days, each season bringing with it its own excitement and event, along with the satisfaction and pride he gained from running an efficient operation in the face of continual difficulty. His letters home, however, were tedious affairs, bald accounts of trade figures, illnesses within the ebb and flow of the community around the lake, lists of births and deaths of people unknown to his correspondents. He was aware of the impression these uninspired missives must create, that of a lonely, sad and bored man with little to interest him and even less to inspire him. He yearned to convey to them the almost daily drama he lived, played out in this land of deprivation and challenge.

Tragedy when the son of one of his regular traders went out alone to hunt his first deer, his initial twelve-year-old step towards manhood. It was the autumn, not yet enough snow to build an igloo but plenty to blow into a fierce ground blizzard. The boy found and killed his caribou about five miles from the post and, filled with pride, he strapped the carcass to his sled and set off into the blizzard with his dog and his kill, anxious to share his good fortune with his family. The storm blew all day and the boy did not come home. Alerted by the family, Sandy and the RCMP man set out to find him. It was impossible. The drifting snow had wiped out all tracks, the wind continued to batter them and in spite of their growing sense of alarm and urgency, forced them to abandon the search until it had abated. They found him the following day a few hundred yards beyond the settlement behind the rise of a hill. Disorientated by a change in the wind direction, he had veered from the proper track he had been following and passed them by. Instead he had fallen and, lying on his back, his eyes and mouth packed with snow, he had frozen to death while his dog lay beside him, gnawing contentedly on the caribou carcass.

Excitement when a Roman Catholic missionary from Repulse Bay out hunting alone fell through the thin ice and struggled for ten minutes in the bitterly cold water until he could pull himself free. He lost a mitten and his right hand quickly became hard and stiff from the frost. Found and helped by passing Inuit, he made it back to his post but there was neither alcohol to wash the frozen hand nor sedatives to ease the agony of thawing flesh. Realising that outside help was needed if his priest's life was to be saved, the senior missionary attempted to contact Churchill where there was air transport and the possibility of a flight to a hospital and safety. But the winter blizzards had started and his transmission could only reach Sandy, who in turn relayed the cry for help.

From then on Sandy kept a heroic vigil by his radio, passing on messages of worsening weather, impossible flying conditions, while the young priest's condition deteriorated. Gangrene set in and the senior priest, using a kitchen knife without any anaesthetic for the patient, cut away pieces of rotting flesh that had turned black. And then, in the face of all odds, three men attempted the mercy flight. It took them ten days, fog and icing, snowstorms grounding them, the continual threat of weather closing in, the lack of navigational landmarks in this vast whiteness. The chances of making it were stacked against them.

Sandy lived this drama with them, hour by hour and day by day as the flight continued. He knew the terrain they were attempting to cross, the endless plain of the Barrens slipping into the sea in long beaches and tide flats. Snow blanketing the frozen sea and land alike under an endless sheet of white. No shadows, no contrast, no sensation of distance from the ground. And always the warning, he communicated, of more weather that could ground them, fling them fatally off course or exhaust their fuel supplies. But they made it, those three courageous men, the pilot, the engineer, the radio operator in their single-engined Junkers monoplane and brought back the young priest to hospital where the doctors saved his hands and his life.

Sandy grinned wryly to himself as he put his name to yet another of his indifferent letters home. He had given them the bones of his news but in its précised form it conveyed none of the heart-stopping drama he had lived. Instead it read like the station report in which he recorded daily the minutiae of life on and around the post for the edification of those at Head Office. He was no writer, he acknowledged – a teller of stories, oh yes, but no writer.

It was time to take home leave at last, he concluded reluctantly. Then he could tell his stories and share his life with his family. It was also time to face up to the problem of Ella.

CHAPTER 26

She had known for weeks that he was on his way but now that his arrival was imminent she found herself in a panic of indecision. It had seemed a cut and dried situation. She would reiterate her demands for either his immediate return to Scotland or a more appropriate posting to somewhere civilized, Montreal or Winnipeg, otherwise their marriage was over and she would seek advice from her lawyer regarding a divorce. Her mother and father had counselled her, all her friends had plied her with unsought advice on what she must do, how firm she must be, how essential it was to snatch the upper ground at the start, showing him she would brook no argument nor compromise.

But now it did not seem so simple. She found herself breathless with the anticipation of his arrival, able to think only of the laughter in his eyes and the gentleness of his voice. She almost ached to feel his arms around her although she shied away from the thought of any further intimacy. She tried on and rejected everything she had in her wardrobe, looking with despair at the image of herself she saw mirrored on the wall and even the outfit she and Florence had shopped for failed to disguise her thickened figure or lighten the sallow unhappy expression that was now permanently etched on her face.

And then he was there, little changed, the blue of his eyes intensified perhaps by his ruddy complexion, but his face was still unlined, the picture of a perfect Scottish gentleman in his Harris tweeds, his trilby hat set at a jaunty angle on his thinning hair. And inwardly she yearned for this man to stay with her. How proud she would be to walk by his side. He had brought them all gifts. Pretty statuettes carved from soapstone, of Eskimo people fishing, hunting, travelling on their sleds. It really was quite impressive art, she heard herself say, for such a primitive people. And she saw his face darken and his mouth turn grim. For her he had brought a necklace, made from the tusks of walrus, he said, very ethnic and not to her taste but she appreciated that he had singled her out with something different and supposed it must have been expensive.

Finally the dinner was over and they were left alone to talk. They sat in the splendid drawing room of her parents' house, the room bathed in a soft pink light from the velvet shades of the occasional lamps around them. There was a nervous silence at first and then they both began to speak at once: Ella of their future together, Sandy, in a pathetic attempt to avoid important issues, of his pleasure at seeing her family again and the warmth of their welcome to him.

"You're right." He took a deep breath. "We have got to talk. It's the main reason I came home, although I couldn't have come earlier, you realize that," he added hastily. "There were too many things to be dealt with to come sooner – William's death, his family to see to," he finished lamely.

Ella sat, outwardly calm but with a turmoil of hopes, of disturbing affection for him and exasperation with him, battling within her.

"Have you come to give me good news, Sandy?" she asked evenly and at his pretended ignorance of her meaning she clucked impatiently and continued, "Have you come to your senses at last and are now prepared to live in civilization either here or in Canada?"

Again a long silence as he looked at her levelly and without dissemblance.

"I intend to stay at Baker Lake, Ella. I'm sorry if I disappoint you. I'm even more sorry if that means we have no future together," he lied, "but there it is. This job, these people, are my life. We understand each other, we depend on each other. I'd be no good at a desk job, Ella. You've read the letters I write, dull dreary affairs. That's because I find writing dull and dreary. I need action. I need the perpetual challenge of the

Arctic. Above all, I need the Inuit. *They* are my family. I've told you all this before. You're hearing nothing new, but again, I'm sorry if my coming home led you to expect something different."

And she knew she was defeated. All the arguments she had prepared, the threats she had intended to issue, they were all to no avail. But perversely, she was encouraged. Deep within her had been the belief that had theirs been a love match, had she been young and beautiful and desirable, she would have persuaded him to live her life. Now she knew, without a shadow of doubt, that his all-abiding love was for that country and those people and no one could come between them.

She also knew, suddenly, that she would keep him. There would be no divorce because she still wanted him, however remote, however long his absences might be, she would remain Mrs. Alexander Lunan. She had no need of his money. Although he provided for her, it was as a drop in the ocean beside the affluence and comfort furnished by her own family. She knew she could live contentedly without him. But his existence as her husband gave her status, respect and, strangely, cloaked her with an aura of romance. She was someone different in their community. Not a woman discarded by her husband but a faithful and patient wife, unable by force of circumstances to join her husband because of the demands of his job and the frailty of her health. There, she had it, the perfect excuse to hold on to him.

To his amazement she nodded, apparently satisfied with his explanation. He had been expecting pleading, tears perhaps, and then anger and bitterness. Instead she half smiled at him and with a cough she placed one hand over her mouth and began again to talk to him, this time as though it were an effort for her to speak.

"You've made your point, Sandy. I appreciate where your heart and your duty lie. And, suspecting already the impossibility of a change in your situation, I was determined to go with you." She paused, attempted to breathe deeply but instead provoked a spasm of coughing that both alarmed and puzzled Sandy. He fetched water for her and then resumed his seat, waiting in bewilderment and not a little consternation for her to continue.

"But it's not to be, my dear." Her eyes refused to meet his and she turned her head, in what he could only think of as dramatic effect. "I consulted my doctor, told him of my plans to follow you to the Arctic, and he tells me I have consumption. I have little enough time as it is but if I went with you I would be dead within months."

There was a stunned silence as Sandy digested this news and then he knelt at her feet, held her hand and told her of his shock and pain at her announcement. She smiled bravely and accepted his comfort and affection. She begged him only to keep her illness a secret between themselves as she did not want to cause her family unnecessary worry and grief.

And then Sandy guessed. She had found the infallible way, the only way, to keep him. He could never accuse her of false-hood, it would be unthinkable to brand her a hypochondriac. Instead they would live this compromise, she keeping her dignity and position as a married woman and he his freedom in all but name. He had come home hoping to resolve the pointless burden of this marriage and now he would go back still tied but with the unspoken understanding that she would no longer expect him to share her life.

It could have been worse, he told himself ruefully after he had bidden her goodnight. They had already started to play the charade of her as an invalid by agreeing it would be best if he returned to his brother's house for the night. She would manufacture some excuse for her parents' benefit, she assured him. He recalled the terrible moment when she had told him she had resolved to return to Baker Lake with him and he had known in an instant that he could not live with this woman. And then the shock and shameful relief when she had revealed her "illness". She had never been attractive to him but the years had been particularly unkind to her and although he had hidden his dismay well he now found her actively disagreeable, a stout, sour and spoilt matron. He was trapped, well and truly, but once he was back in the world he knew best all this would be only an unpleasant memory, far removed from reality.

He spent the rest of his leave moving between Carnoustie, where most of his sisters lived, and Edinburgh to where Aggie had returned following the untimely death of Bill, her husband, in Canada. She now had two children, Janet and Billy, the niece and nephew he felt most drawn to, and in spite of the unfortunate and unforeseen beginning to his leave, he found, for the most part, he had enjoyed this holiday in his home land. His friendship with Dom remained a steady and uncomplicated pleasure enhanced now by the addition of a delightful and growing family of impossibly beautiful bambinos. But it was nevertheless a great relief to him to board his ship back to Canada. Europe was rumbling again with the warnings of unrest and impending disaster. It was time to bury himself again in the cold but comforting isolation of the north.

CHAPTER 27

Hekwaw brought back his death with him from Chesterfield Inlet. He had visited the station with his dog sled, compelled by curiosity rather than any need, to see the white man's town and all its marvels for himself. And he was greatly impressed. Here was an airport into which flew planes of all shapes and sizes, there were buildings, more than he had ever seen. Why did they need so many, what secrets did they contain? But most of all he marvelled at the people. So many and all of them it seemed in a hurry to get somewhere, do something. But some of them had time for him, as fascinated, it would seem, by his strangeness to them as they were to him. Some of the young men from the airfield befriended him, communicated with him by signs and smiles, admired his clothes and his dogs, gave him food and gifts of tobacco and a fiery liquid they called rum.

Unknown to all, however, they gave him one more gift, unwanted and deadly – influenza.

He was already sick by the time he returned to Akumalik, Martee and Nilak, who were with the rest of the family group camped now in snow houses about five miles from the HBC trading post. Quickly the germs spread, taking hold in the lungs of those who had no tolerance to disease, who were helpless in the face of this unknown and terrifying illness. The babies were the first to die and then the old people, while Hekwaw clung to life, his fever burning him and his body weakened as he rejected the food and liquid he needed to fight and win. Akumalik was frantic. She nursed him and comforted him but, instinctively fearing the worst and in an effort to protect her daughter and son from the infection, she sent Nilak to the place of the white men to seek help.

By the time Sandy reached the settlement it was too late. In spite of Akumalik's tireless ministrations and the invocations of the shaman called by her to exorcise the evil spirits that inhabited his body, Hekwaw coughed up his life blood and died. His death was the last. The disease had run its course and although all Sandy could do was to bring supplies, brew tea, make soup and stew to nourish exhausted bodies, his coming coincided with recovery and the Inuit thanked him and marvelled at his powers.

It was the first time Akumalik had seen the Red One. Saddened by the death of her husband but overpoweringly grateful that the life of her daughter and Nilak had been spared, she fingered the necklace that she kept always next to her skin and watched as he organised and comforted, restoring order to lives that had been devastated by tragedy and terrified by the unknown. She saw his kindness and knew that this new horror they had endured he had made his own. He grieved with them in their loss but urged them to put their terror behind them as, he explained, this fatal sickness was unlikely to visit them again. He spoke eventually to her, asking how she would manage now that her husband had died and she no longer had someone to provide for her and her daughter. His accent was strange but he spoke her language well.

"You are the widow of Hekwaw, are you not?" he asked gently. She nodded dumbly, a wave of sadness at her recent loss catching at her throat and bringing a momentary prickling behind her eyes.

"Then you are the maker of these!" He gestured at his parka and the caribou-skin trousers he was wearing, his face now alight with a smile that warmed and coaxed a shy acknowledgement from her.

"I was never able to thank you for your work but I do now and as you can see, your sewing has stood the test of time. These clothes are as good now as when you first made them. You have a fine talent."

They grinned at each other, she inordinately gratified by his compliments, he enjoying her pleasure and then suddenly struck by an idea that became an urgent desire as soon as he had formulated it.

"I need a housekeeper. Someone to cook for me and young Alistair, my new clerk, and to keep the house in order. We've been managing for a while on our own with a bit of help from time to time from the storeman's wife. But he has decided to leave us at Baker Lake to join a family group out trapping. Sensible man," he muttered more to himself than to her, "keeping alive his traditional skills rather than depend on the bounty of the white man. You would live out, of course," he added hastily, "with your son and daughter. He could learn to help in the store if you liked. And best of all, I will know where to find you when I need another set of furs!"

Akumalik looked at him in amazement. It was too much for her to comprehend, it was too sudden. She had avoided Kabluna, the white men, all her life and now here was one, the Red One, offering her food and security, comfort and employment for her, Martee and Nilak. But in return she would have to tailor her life to his, forfeit her nomadic ways, learn the procedures that fashioned his lifestyle. She hesitated only a moment.

"I will be happy to look after you and the clerk," she replied simply. "Thank you."

Sandy went about his business absurdly pleased with himself. He felt instinctively he had brought about a coup. This woman would be perfect, he told himself. If she could cook as well as she could sew they would be fortunate indeed. And she was so dignified. She held herself well, he mused, and looked you straight in the eye, none of this coy giggling and flirting you got with a lot of the young women with whom he came in contact. The boy Nilak could also be of benefit to them. He appeared to be bright and sensible. He had delivered the message of sickness of his family without hysteria and had worked well and efficiently with him and Alistair as they had loaded their sleds with supplies to aid his stricken relatives. Old enough to learn quickly yet young enough to train to his own methods without question. How old would he be? The facial hair was apparent already – about sixteen Sandy guessed. But his mother was still a young woman. My god, he thought, unaware that Nilak was in fact her stepson, she must have been only a child herself when she had that baby and now she was already a widow. Perhaps this was the secret of her strange self-assurance. She had never known a proper childhood. She had taken on the responsibilities of motherhood so early.

He checked himself. What was the matter with him? What did it matter what her history concealed as long as she did her job well and only spoke when it was necessary? Women, in his experience, were compulsive talkers. That would not do at all. But she would be different, of that he was sure.

Her future now assured, Akumalik prepared for the death rituals of her husband. His body remained in their snow house on the sleeping platform for days and during that time she was forbidden to sew, his male relatives to saw or hammer and no bones of the caribou could be broken to get at the marrow. She remained with him throughout that harrowing period, sharing the sleeping platform with his lifeless body, now frozen stiff as heat inside the snow house would have caused decomposition.

At last, at the end of the four days, she forced his limbs, with enormous difficulty, into his cleanest clothes and then wrapped him in deerskins, lashing the thongs tightly to prevent the body from escaping. He was carried to the sled with his head pointing in the direction they would travel to his 'burial' place. But there could be no burial, the ground as yet unbending in its winter freeze. Akumalik now silently said her final goodbye to the man who had cared for her these last sixteen years, the father of her daughter, a good man. She felt grief in her loss but she had seen so much death, had now narrowly escaped for the second time her own death, that she was fatalistic about his going.

Nilak, with his two uncles, would take the sled to the place that long ago Hekwaw had designated his. They would place his body with its head pointing to the west and then circle it three times. Nilak would make a small hole in the caribou skins near his father's head. Now the soul could escape, the soul that would wander near its earthly body until a new-born baby took the name Hekwaw. Then it would be still and bother the living no more.

Akumalik would not visit the burial place of her husband. She had no wish to encounter his spirit and she knew his body would be claimed quickly by the wandering wolves and foxes. But she knew where he had been taken and she knew that forever it would be known as *Hekwaw iluvra*, Hekwaw's resting place.

She told the group of her decision to stay by the Hudson's Bay post and there was general agreement that she had been lucky and wise to take up the Red One's offer. She sensed relief amongst them that she would no longer be their responsibility, although she knew they would always be her family and would visit her when they came to trade. She thought briefly with trepidation of her future and then she put her worries behind her. She, Martee and Nilak would be fine. The Red One would see to that.

CHAPTER 28

1940 and while the second war to end all wars raged around
the world, Sandy existed in relative isolation in his own king-
dom in the Arctic. He followed its progress on his radio and
there were many days when, depressed and alarmed at the latest set-back for the British, fighting alone, it seemed, a doomed
battle against the Third Reich, his face remained grim and he
was curt and ill-tempered with those around him.

Akumalik wanted to understand. Alistair attempted to explain about the madness that was happening far far away, people killing each other in their thousands and the ones Sandy and
Alistair liked were losing. But it was difficult for her to comprehend. There seemed to be food enough for all, the ship that
brought their supplies still came, why was there fighting when
starvation and survival were not apparently the problem? Sandy,
listening to Alistair's bewildering explanation, attempted to enlighten. He knew she had no concept of number, having lived
with and encountered only small family groups her whole life.

"You know when your hunters follow the caribou, when
the year is good and tuktu comes, many animals. And although
the hunters kill, again and again, still tuktu comes, sometimes for
days you can hear the drumming of the hooves on the tundra?"
Akumalik nodded, smiling at the memory of good times.

"Well, there are people, as many as the deer out there, and
although there is killing many more take their place and survive.
There will always be people out there. We will not be alone."

But it was more difficult to explain why the fighting was
taking place. Territorial acquisition was an unknown concept to
her and he could only mutter lamely that it was a sort of blood
feud that his 'family' had with another group; that this enemy

threatened their existence and it was essential that his 'family' win. It was an unsatisfactory and inaccurate metaphor, he realized, even as he fashioned it, but he could think of no other and it seemed at least to satisfy her.

Sandy was affected directly in one way by the war. HBC had all its planes, except for two kept back for emergencies and first aid duties, requisitioned by the government for the war effort, necessitating greater reliance on the dog sleds and increased basic inventory levels. To this end he was seconded to Churchill for three months in the summer to help with the planning and coordinating of the Company's transportation requirements.

It was here that he met Scotty, the half-breed son of an HBC manager and his Inuik housekeeper at Bathurst Inlet. Sandy knew that, although never openly condoned by the company, it was a well-known and recognized fact that there were many managers who took native women to their beds to comfort them, especially in areas of desolation and loneliness. But he had often wondered what the offspring of such a union could expect from life. Scotty volunteered the information with a frankness that had dispelled immediately Sandy's initial embarrassment about questioning him on such a private matter. To Scotty, it would seem, had been given advantages from both his parents. His mother had been envied in their settlement because the white manager had preferred her to the other young women. And when his father had left, transferred to another HBC outpost, he was loved equally and without discrimination by his mother, her family and his half brothers and sisters who she subsequently had by an Inuik husband. His father had remained in touch and because of his influence and the fact that he, Scotty, spoke the white man's language, he had been given this splendid job with the Company in Churchill. He was fortunate indeed, he assured Sandy.

It was an interesting assessment, Sandy thought. He mused briefly on what a child of his would look like. Say with someone like… Akumalik. Presumably it would have her features.

That seemed to be the case with half-breeds. They favoured the Inuik facial characteristics but there was the chance his eyes and his colouring could prevail. Quite a fascinating combination. He suddenly realized what he was doing and mentally chided himself for the ridiculousness of the exercise. He and Akumalik! What nonsense! All the same, he missed her down here. Just because of her cooking, of course. It would be good to get home again. No one made his porridge the way she did.

CHAPTER 29

Akumalik adapted to life among the white men with an ease that surprised her. At first she was frightened. Her existence up to this time, although often precarious and fraught with potential disaster, had been unformed, hours filled with the day-to-day tasks of living but with no set structure or urgency. Meals were made when people were hungry and meat was available. Sleep was taken when one was tired, at any time – the Arctic months varying from almost total darkness to the never-setting sun. Sometimes, when blizzards raged for days on end and hunting was impossible, the families slept or dozed waiting for the winds and snows to abate, conserving energy and heat until it was possible to operate safely again.

Now, suddenly, her days were bound by clocks and timetables and hungry men needing pre-planned meals. And Sandy, she was warned at the outset by his anxious assistant, was a stickler when it came to time-keeping. It took only two mistakes before she began to learn and adjust to his ways and, although he neither shouted nor scolded, the obvious displeasure on his face when she kept him waiting for his meal was reason enough, she resolved, to avoid causing him further disappointment.

Nilak found it more difficult. With the arrogance of youth, he regularly turned up late at the store where Alistair and sometimes Sandy were attempting to teach him his duties. When chastised, gently at first, he shrugged his indifference and deliberately repeated his misconduct the following morning. This time he was warned. But on the third morning Akumalik heard Sandy's anger from the house. She wisely forced herself to remain in the kitchen although all her instincts screamed at her to rush to her son's defence. Instead she determined to speak to Nilak alone that night to counsel and persuade his obedience.

There was no need. The Red One had made his point in no uncertain terms and Nilak had no wish to suffer a repeat performance. He was, from then on, a punctual and able pupil and mother and son learned quickly that there was often an eventual self-revealing logic to Sandy's sometimes bewildering ways.

Their training programme had scarcely begun, however, when Sandy's three-month secondment to Churchill took place and Akumalik found herself in charge at the station house with only Alistair, an altogether easier subject to please, to feed and look after. It was a fortuitous breathing space for her. It gave her time to adjust to her new and strange life without the constant worry of causing upset. Alistair coached her, not in her household duties, which she had mastered with no difficulty, but in the mysteries of Sandy's likes and dislikes. They appeared to be multitudinous. Often she would ask why but his answer was always the same. "Because that's the way he likes it. He's set in his ways you know." She was quickly aware that Alistair had a deep affection for the older man without necessarily understanding him.

Her days had a placid sameness and she settled into the rhythm of routine happily. And then, with the end of summer, he came back and she was disconcerted by the leap her heart made at the first sight of him. She decided it was anxiety. Again she would have to watch herself, make sure she and Nilak toed the line. She turned back into the kitchen after the first welcoming smiles were over and did not see Sandy's puzzled frown at the sound of banging pots and pans. It was a nuisance, she told herself, all these petty rules and regulations; they were so much more relaxed while he was away.

But strangely it was also a comfort to hear his rough greeting in the morning as she placed before him the almost sacred bowl of porridge, oats which she had soaked the previous night and brought to a steady slow boil to be ready for him at 6.45am precisely. It was not a good idea to attempt conversation at this time and she learned to keep a watchful but silent presence in the background. Then he and Alistair would go about their various chores while she washed and polished, making tea throughout the morning and watching with amusement as Sandy's mood improved as the hours progressed.

He spent a lot of his time at a desk in an alcove in the living room, his reading glasses perched on the end of his nose, shuffling papers and writing things, a task that Akumalik thought would have been boring in the extreme but which seemed to give him a certain pleasure. There would be grunts of satisfaction as he bundled yet another sheaf of papers together and stacked them tidily with all the others he had dealt with, ready to go wherever to whoever.

Taking and sending messages on the radio also consumed a good portion of his time but if news of the war was bad or if someone, far away, in the Company demanded something he considered a waste of time, his temper was uncertain and Akumalik kept her distance. He did not shout at her but she did not like to see him distressed and the urge to hold and comfort him out of his mood, as she did with Nilak, was alarming. Far better to distract herself with cleaning or mending until it was time for another mug-up and she would be rewarded with a courteous thank-you and his special smile as she handed him his cup of tea.

He was rarely discontented at dinner time. Sandy relished his food and had been particularly complimentary about her cooking skills. She baked excellent bread, her caribou stew was second to none, he told her frequently, and once she had grasped the idea of punctuality she frequently basked in his fulsome praise. He always changed for dinner, out of the skins and parka that he wore during the day, into grey slacks and an immaculate tweed jacket. In her eyes he now became so much more the white man, so foreign, his eyes somehow bluer, his complexion more florid. And yet she liked him like this. He fascinated her.

They often had guests – the policemen from the R.C.M.P.

base, visiting weathermen, geologists or scientists, botanists exploring the unique flora and fauna of the Arctic. He seemed to blossom in company, become animated in conversation and was obviously a successful raconteur, judging by the gales of laughter that rocked the table and echoed through to her kitchen. He always introduced her to his guests. The frequent visitors who lived at the settlement became her friends and although she could not speak nor understand any of the white man's language, he would take the time after they had gone to explain their business to her, help her to appreciate the importance of their work. Her horizons broadened and her knowledge deepened.

Ship time arrived shortly after Sandy returned from Churchill and with it a frantic activity at the station but, even more exciting to Akumalik, the arrival of groups of Inuit, amongst them her friends and family, who were anxious to help with the loading and unloading and make their autumn trade. They pitched their tents around the HBC storehouse and on the shores of the lake and then came to visit. Sandy always had time for the Inuit. They came into the Eskimo room and sat chatting with him, telling of their latest hardships or triumphs, the deaths or births which had occurred since they last saw him, a juicy piece of gossip or the marvels performed by the local shaman who had brought his spirits to heal, to make a woman fertile, to give a man strength and skill for the hunt. Sandy knew them all by name. He knew their wives and their children, he knew of their bereavements and their marriages. Akumalik brought in kettles of tea, hardtack biscuits and there was much noise and laughter and genuine good feeling. She had her own party in her tent while those she had lived with as Hekwaw's wife asked innumerable questions about her new life. As is the way with the Inuit, they asked the most personal of questions. Had he, the white man, taken her to his bed yet and if not, who was his woman? She was unaccountably upset by their curiosity and offended by their interest. Her denial was abrupt and quick, discouraging further good-natured probing and vulgar hilarity.

Instead she diverted their interest to the many new things she had learned and soon she had their astonished attention as she told of the white man's war and of the amazing disembodied voices that came from his radio.

Then the ship came and everyone helped. She made endless mug-ups while men, women and children trudged back and forth from the beach to the warehouses, ferrying the cases and boxes and bales from the ship and loading up the returning barges with huge bundles of caribou and fox fur pelts. The deer skins would be shipped to the coastal ports of the Arctic where the Inuit had little access to the migratory herds of caribou and needed the skins for clothing and bedding. There was a moment of panic when Sandy realized his liquor supply for the year had not yet been unloaded and Alistair was dispatched immediately on the next barge to retrieve the precious cargo from the captain's cabin. It took two days to complete the unloading and at the end all were numb with an aching weariness, adrenaline exhausted. But there was a quiet satisfaction in the station house that night and Akumalik felt she shared in their achievement. She knew her friends would be packing their tents soon for their fall hunting and trapping grounds but she knew she would not fret to see them go, nor wish to go with them. It was extraordinary how quickly she had become part of this white man's world and how comfortable she felt in it.

CHAPTER   30

There was a rap at the door and Sandy straightened, took his glasses off his nose and let the newspaper he was reading slip down by the side of his chair.

"Is that someone wanting in, lad?" he asked Alistair.

Barely able to contain his amusement, the young clerk nodded dumbly, opened the door and stood back to admit the black-suited, dog-collared Anglican minister.

"Well hello, Mr. James, hello. How are you?" A flourish as Sandy got to his feet and indicated a seat for the missionary.

"Well good evening, Mr. Lunan. I just happened to be passing by and I thought I'd drop in for a moment."

Alistair covered his mirth by busying himself with the rum bottle and a glass for the minister. It was a scene replayed almost every Sunday since he had been at Baker Lake and, if his predecessor were to be believed, for many years beforehand. Always the look of surprise on Sandy's face when the open door revealed Jimmy James, always the suggestion of a chance visit by the minister although he turned up regularly week after week on the dot of seven. It mystified Alistair why the two men were so formal with each other when everyone else called them both by their Christian names but when he had asked he received only a frown from Sandy that warned him to mind his own business. He was left to assume that their behaviour was either a mutual respect between them which they demonstrated with outmoded Victorian courtesy or an unease between them which they cloaked with formality. Alistair tended to the latter explanation. He had heard Sandy's views on Christianity and its proselytising messengers. Anyway, what did it matter. After dinner he left them to their conversation and went to his own room to read.

Aupaluktuk - the Red One

The two older men chatted amiably about the weather, events at the settlement, until a clatter from the kitchen distracted them both and Jimmy James changed the subject.

"A fine looking woman," he remarked laconically, his broad Northumberland accent carrying an uncommon note of approval as he acknowledged Akumalik's presence in the background.

"Can't say I've noticed," lied Sandy as he fiddled nervously with his cigarette packet and lit a rare sixth smoke. He rationed himself normally to five a day and smoked them all in the evening. "But she's a good cook and housekeeper." He heard himself prattle on: "...and the boy has turned out well after a few hiccups at the start. He's a grand help in the store, gives Alistair a hand grading the hides, handles the dogs well and has started to set trap lines in the lake so we get a regular fish diet too. He..."

"Carries herself with dignity," continued the minister as though Sandy had not spoken at all. Sandy stared, momentarily silenced. He remembered suddenly an old story he had been told by Archie Hunter, a former HBC manager, of Jimmy James' home leave which he had announced would be for the sole purpose of finding a wife. Nothing had been said by anyone when the tall gloomy minister had returned unaccompanied and it was assumed his mission had been a failure. Sandy had been amused by the story. He'd previously thought the man a natural virgin but "still waters run deep," he had commented at the time and perhaps it was still true. Perhaps the minister was a seething mass of sexual repression. Sandy grew unaccountably irritable.

"You should get yourself a good housekeeper," he snapped. "There are usually one or two youngsters or widows who come in with the trading groups who could use the employment. Takes some of the burden of responsibility from their families. They don't all adapt, of course. Take badly to the white man's life. We've been lucky with Akumalik," he said firmly, stressing the collective article.

"I haven't seen her at the services though," mused the minister. "Don't suppose you know whether she goes to the opposition?"

Of course, thought Sandy, engulfed by an inexplicable relief. He wants to add her to his army of the saved. There's nothing sinister at all in his interest. A one-track mind seems to come with the 'seeing of the light', poor soul. Then he felt an anger build up as he recognized with dislike the missionary zeal.

"She has her own faith and it serves a far better purpose than the white man's imported beliefs. So get any ideas of conversion or baptism out of your head, she has no time for it," he growled, aware that his abruptness bordered on rudeness and also uncomfortably conscious that he had no knowledge of her religious tendencies nor had he any right to speak on her behalf.

Further tetchy discussion was brought to a close as the clock on the mantle started a familiar whirr preparatory to striking the hour. Jimmy James leapt to his feet with almost indecent haste.

"Well this has been very pleasant, Mr. Lunan, but I must be getting back to the church. I've a bit of writing to do before turning in."

Right on the dot of ten, thought Sandy. Always seems to leave about the same time but just as well, I could do with my bed. It did not occur to him that his bedtime was well documented with those at the post and the minister would no more have braved staying past the witching hour than he would have asked Sandy to attend his church services. With a token reluctance he saw the minister to the door and yawning turned back into the house and wandered through to the kitchen, startling both himself and Akumalik who had come back quietly into the house to wash up the two glasses and empty Sandy's cigarette butts from the ashtray. It was cosy and warm in the kitchen which was heated by the cooking range and Akumalik's face was flushed a rosy pink, her eyes wide with the surprise of seeing him still up after the clock had struck ten. She normally wore her hair in a long braid down her back but she had loosened it by now and it shone richly in the soft light of the paraffin lamp. Unable to stop himself, Sandy reached out his hand and stroked it, shocked equally at the irrationality of his gesture and by the silken texture he felt beneath his finger. She stood like a statue, transfixed by his touch. Then, as though stung, he withdrew his hand and turned away abruptly.

"It's pretty, your hair," she heard him mutter gruffly as he stamped out of the kitchen and into his bedroom.

It was the devil's own job to compose himself for sleep that night. Try as he might he could not banish the image of Akumalik from his mind and Jimmy James' comments on her handsomeness replayed themselves with irritating frequency. He was alternatively disconcerted that the man had voiced such thoughts about his housekeeper and amazed that the minister had recognized her qualities before he had. Of course he had noticed her looks, he told himself, just never acknowledged that she was, well, so womanly, he supposed. He always felt good around her. She had a habit of looking you straight in the eye that he admired and she had the sense to ask if she was unsure what was expected of her. Didn't just muddle through and hope for the best like many he knew. But, come to think of it, he had probably never really looked at her before tonight. Just been aware and pleased that she was there. Anyway, what did it matter what she looked like?

He turned on his side and thumped his pillow, as long as she did her job well. But, she was a bonny little thing, there was no doubt about that. He smiled to himself in the darkness. Quite a feather in his cap, he supposed, having a housekeeper everyone else admired. He remembered now the outrageous way the policemen flirted with her when they came over for dinner. He'd never given it any thought before except to be mildly amused by the way she deftly countered their overtures. But perhaps that was all show. The thought was enough to bring him instantly awake again. Perhaps she was creeping out of that tent of hers into someone's bed every night after he had gone to sleep. She was a young woman, she had been a wife and had given and received intimacies since she was a girl. She would be missing that side of her life.

He worried away at the thought for what seemed to be most of the night but eventually fell into a fitful and unsatisfactory sleep. The next morning he woke unrefreshed and petulant and surprised both Alistair and Akumalik with an uncharacteristic display of ill humour over the texture of his porridge. Much too lumpy, he grumbled and pushed it aside only half eaten. Alistair shrugged, raised his eyebrows at Akumalik in perplexed mystification and went about his work.

But Akumalik was hurt. She had fallen asleep hugging to herself the amazing thought of his hand on her hair and the momentary softness she had seen in his eyes. And now he was angry with her. There was nothing wrong with the porridge, she finished it off herself later to satisfy herself of its consistency. He was just a bad-tempered old man, she decided, and not worth another thought. But there was much banging of doors and clattering of pots in the kitchen that day and both men were relieved to escape into the cold and quiet of the store.

CHAPTER   31

Winter came again and with it the hundred and one jobs of maintenance that were neglected during the heavy trading times. The company buildings had to be painted and repaired, the ravages caused by weather seemingly endless. The preparation of their home brew was another vital bad-weather occupation. As post manager Sandy was allocated only two twelve-bottled crates a year, one of whisky and one of rum, so their own concoction was essential to eke out supplies. Akumalik, Martee and Nilak packed up their summer tent and built their snowhouse. "Probably a lot warmer than we are in here, lad," commented Sandy when Alistair voiced his concern for their comfort.

Dark days and black nights for months on end often with blizzards raging day after day bring a keen sense of isolation, loneliness and despair. Sandy had run the gamut of these emotions all too often during his years in the Arctic and knew how important it was to keep busy, to keep to a schedule. Once slackness set in morale deteriorated. An unhappy situation anywhere, the breakdown of discipline here could lead to madness and, on occasion, death. Sandy had seen men degenerate from lazy indolent creatures, lolling about without purpose to crazy lunatics, crying for the return of the sun and escape from their interminable night. He knew he often irritated those he commanded with his, to their minds, petty attention to detail, insistence upon punctuality. But these trifling inconveniences he visited upon them were, in their way, life-savers. Life at his post was as structured during the frightening endlessness of winter as it was through the enjoyable activity of the other seasons.

Christmas, and a big party at the post for any Inuit in the area, the white man celebrating his religious festival and the native a sighting of Aagyuluk, a star formation that heralds the imminent arrival of the sun on the horizon again, a promise that the long dark days of winter have reached a turning point and summer will eventually come. There was a drum dance, a time when memories are revisited, stories and legends of the People told, the words of the songs as important as the fevered beating of the drum and the rhythm of the dance. Each person had his or her own story to tell, of a great hunt, of a time of starvation, and the singer sways to the unique compulsion of his composition while the dancers leap to their feet, listening to the story and moving to the throbbing primitive lure of the drum. It was a provocative performance, often sexual, and Sandy left early, pleading a tiredness he did not feel but unable to witness any longer the heady scene dispassionately. There was an unaccountable answering urge in him that caused him physical and mental discomfort. He decided the batch of home brew he had sampled earlier that night had been too strong and he switched on his radio deliberately forcing himself back to the real world, the"civilised" world he told himself ironically, of war and disaster. The celebrations carried on, wild and exciting and without him.

CHAPTER 32

Early July, a day as perfect as the brief Arctic summers allows, found Sandy working on a pile of invoices at his desk in the house. Outside the sun sparkled on the lake, the open water free of the ice banks that still partly restricted its shoreline, and the surrounding tundra jewelled with the myriads of tiny flowers nodding gently in a soft breeze. He was alone in the house, Alistair on a four-day hunting expedition with Nilak, and Akumalik off duty and presumably occupied with something in her tent. It was hot, and in an effort to benefit from any movement of air Sandy had taken off his brushed cotton shirt that now hung over the back of his chair. He sat in an incongruous informality in his singlet, the pale flesh of his chest and arms in stark contrast to the ruddy weather-beaten geography of his face.

There was a sudden commotion from outside. Shouting, urgency, alarm. Sandy grabbed his shirt and made for the door, buttoning and tucking in the garment as he ran. People were running to the lake-shore from all directions but most stood helplessly once they reached the water and gazed out to a further point in the lake where Sandy could see an overturned kayak and the frantic splashing of people trying to stay afloat. Dogs tethered to fuel drums that littered the shoreline barked and leapt excitedly, straining at their traces, eager to be part of the obvious drama.

Two Inuit men ran back to their tent and returned with their own kayak. Quickly they launched it into the water. But Sandy plunged headlong in to the icy lake, hardly registering the immediate heart-stopping chill that enveloped his whole body. He swam quickly and accurately reaching the endangered men at the same time as the other kayak. Shouting above the confusion around him he encouraged the one man who was able to tread water and together they heaved his drowning companion into the rescue kayak. Then they righted the overturned craft and pushed it awkwardly towards the shore. It was a lengthy process as Sandy now had to support the other man who appeared to have forgotten how to swim once the immediate danger had passed.

By the time they reached the beach many had waded in and added their strength to the rescue mission but again it was Sandy who took over as they placed the half-conscious man, under his instruction, in the recovery position. He pumped away on his chest, performing artificial resuscitation until water spouted from his mouth and the first signs of life returned as he spluttered and gasped for breath. Immediately there were noisy indications of relief and happiness as the spectators shouted their congratulations, patted him heartily on the back and beamed their thanks and gratitude.

But by now Sandy was beyond the euphoria of his success. Exhaustion had set in and a shivering reaction to the freezing waters he had plunged into without hesitation. But worse than that, far worse, was the appearance of a torturous malevolent cloud of stinging black fly and mosquito that now hung above him, around him, enveloping him in its maddening painful attack. He had forgotten, in his haste to answer the call for help, one of the cardinal rules of the Arctic. He had left the house without the protective clothing that was required in summer as armour against these very predators. Because he had taken off his shirt inside the house his instinctive urge to cover himself before leaving the house had been fooled by the act of putting on his shirt. Now he was at the centre of their attention as they attacked him in their hundreds of thousands, biting and stinging, unable to penetrate the caribou skin jackets and hoods of the Inuit who surrounded him. He swung wildly around him, ducking and swerving in a futile attempt to ward off their attack but it served only to send the watching Inuit into gales of laughter as they saw his insane dance as a celebratory and comic demonstration for their amusement. Driven wild he could only summon the last reserves of his energy and with the attendant black cloud buzzing about him stumble painfully away from the beach and into the safety of his house. Inevitably thousands of the insects entered with him but they were in manageable numbers and were quickly dispatched. He sank to the floor sobbing his relief.

The door opened again and in walked Akumalik. Saying nothing, she crossed the room and kneeling on the floor in front of him began gently to strip the blood-spattered shirt from his back. Too tired to protest, Sandy allowed her ministrations as he now shivered violently from the shock and toxin of the attacks. She fetched warm water with which she washed his bruised flesh, his face and body now swelling visibly, and dabbed with a soothing lotion at his bites. Neither of them spoke although Sandy smiled his thanks as she handed him a clean cotton shirt and left with the basin, the water inside red with his blood.

She had been on the beach as he had waded out of the freezing water and began his life-saving action on the half-drowned man. She had watched with the others as he had made the miracle happen and the man breathe again but she alone had not joined in the innocent laughter of the others as they enjoyed his impromptu dance. She had felt, at that moment, a surge of emotion that was almost suffocating in its intensity. It was something she had never encountered although she knew that similar but less intense sensations had visited her before, all of them connected with Sandy.

She remembered his visit to Churchill and her confusion upon his return and she knew now, with certainty, that his presence brought her happiness. Love was not a word she was familiar with. She knew she felt differently about people. Hekwaw, her husband, she had felt comfortable with, had been grateful to for his support and protection, and she had enjoyed the physical side of her marriage. Martee, her daughter, and

Nilak held a special place within her. She knew she would willingly die for them. But what she felt for Sandy was so different from anything she had known. It threatened to engulf her, to turn her reason, to cause her pain when he was displeased or unhappy or even absent from her for any length of time. But it also gave her moments of supreme joy when her pride in him and her concern for him shut out anything and everyone else. This was enough. It was now clear to her what she must do.

The long Arctic twilight began and at last Sandy was alone again. After Akumalik's ministrations he had begun to recover and was able to receive the steady stream of well-wishers who had either witnessed his heroism or had been told of it. He quickly tired of all the acclaim and was embarrassed by the attention and praise he engendered. He knew he had acted instinctively, anyone would have done the same he assured his audience, it was just fortunate that he could swim, an accomplishment the white man usually learned in childhood. But he had done more than that they insisted. He had brought their friend back from the dead. They had not known that he, the Red One, was a shaman. What other magic could he perform? In the end it was pointless to protest. He smiled modestly and thanked them for their visit but indicated firmly that it was now time for him to sleep. They left reluctantly and he guessed uncomfortably that he was already the stuff of legend.

It had been quite a day he mused as he lay, physically exhausted but mentally very much awake, upon his bed. The bites still itched but the lotion Akumalik had used had taken the worst of the heat away and the attack he had endured was mostly an unpleasant memory, a mistake never to be repeated, a lesson very sorely learned. Akumalik. He allowed himself to think of her. Recently he had found himself thinking of her at the most unsuitable of times and he had disciplined himself to black out the image of her smiling face with something more mundane and appropriate. But today was an exception. She had been so kind, so gentle, so close to him. He had been ashamed of his antics under the insect assault. He knew he had looked ridiculous and had warranted the laughter of the Inuit but the stinging had been unmerciful, unendurable and the very numbers of the creatures had created a panic that was almost approaching terror. She had seen him at his most vulnerable as he lay on the floor, sobbing with the pain and the shock. She had not spoken pointless words of comfort that would have only served to embarrass him, but, with the gentleness of a mother, or a lover, had soothed and cooled him with her touch. Her movements had been caresses. God, how he wanted her. Finally he acknowledged what he had known unconsciously for months. And almost as though he had conjured up his dream, she was there before him. In the half light she stood in the doorway, her long black hair shining like slippery satin around her shoulders, her small shapely form faintly visible beneath a thin cotton shift. He sat up abruptly, startling her with the sudden movement and involuntarily she took a step backwards.

"No, don't go," he whispered and held out his arms towards her. She smiled her lovely smile and moved into his embrace.

CHAPTER 33

The next morning he woke knowing something amazing had happened but momentarily unable to recall it. And then he remembered. Akumalik and the comfort and passion and absolute rightness of her in his arms. He opened his eyes eager to look at her, half hoping she would still be sleeping and that he could enjoy her face and body in repose, defenceless, seeing only her and no reflection of her waking response to him, to anyone. But there was no one there. No one lay next to him and the part of the bed and pillow that had faintly retained her shape was cold. He wondered suddenly if he had imagined, had dreamed even, everything. He smiled slowly to himself. No, she had done the proper thing. It would not do for her to be found in his bed, even in the house at this time in the morning. They had not talked of the consequences of their lovemaking last night. They had barely talked at all. Just murmurs, endearments, expressions of wonder at the feel and touch of each other. But without being told, before he even had the sense to think of, let alone to judge their situation realistically, she had made her own decisions, the right ones.

He washed and dressed leisurely. He was mildly interested to see that the bites that had caused him such pain yesterday and, in a roundabout way, had occasioned such ultimate pleasure, had left only tiny red marks upon his skin like the speckled pattern found on the caps of certain toadstools, angry and indicative of poison. He heard noises in the house and then the sound of Alistair's voice greeting Akumalik. He opened the bedroom door and went in to the kitchen.

"You're back early, lad. I thought you were to be gone another day?"

Waiting for the reply he dared to look towards the stove where Akumalik was standing, vigorously stirring his porridge.

"Yes. We had meant to stay out longer but we ran into an early herd of caribou – sitting ducks they were, and before we knew it we had shot more than we could transport back. It was good luck in a way but it was all too easy. Did us out of the sport."

She had turned now towards him and wishing him good morning placed his bowl on the table. Everything was as it always had been, except perhaps a special warmth in her eyes? He felt a sudden urge to take her in his arms and kiss her. He realized that Alistair was looking at him expectantly.

"What? Sorry, I wasn't paying attention," murmured Sandy, flustered.

"I said," repeated the young man with amusement, "we heard there was a new shaman at the post. Brings people back from the dead and then does his own special magic dance. Very entertaining it is too. Seems like we missed all the fun."

Sandy huffed with embarrassment and turned to his breakfast, listening with half an ear to Alistair's chatter while marvelling at the ease with which Akumalik had handled what could have been an awkward moment for them both.

"You can huff and puff all you like," continued Alistair, "but you've started quite a stir with this raising of the dead thing. I know about it already because yesterday we met a band of Inuit on their way from the post and it was all they could talk about. They will meet up with their family group and the word will spread like wildfire. Before we know it you'll be in demand to heal the sick, perform magic tricks, intercede with the spirits."

"Heal the sick! What do you think I spend half my life doing! They give you a cursory training in first aid when you're an apprentice, a box of bandages and pills when you take over a station post and with that and a massive amount of good luck you are expected to be an Albert Schweitzer. On top of that you have to run your station, look after pesky scientists and weather people who visit and give no thought to the extra rations it takes to feed them while they poke about up here, keep minute records of births and deaths, marriages, caribou migrations. You name it, Winnipeg want to know when anyone so much as hiccups up here. Anyway," he halted in mid-bluster, "I can't think what all the fuss is about. I've 'healed' before. Given out massive doses of antibiotics and stopped some of the flu epidemics."

"Ah yes," chaffed Alistair, "but you've never actually brought a man back from the dead before. Those two natives who we met actually saw the dead man hauled out of the kayak and then you pumped his chest, blew in his mouth and all the bad spirits flew out of his mouth in a gush of water." He stood grinning at Sandy as he watched the older man rise from his chair in exasperation, unable to gainsay the Inuits' logic.

There was a rattle at the door and a group of Inuit stood there in deputation.

"Tell them we'll open the store in five minutes," muttered Sandy. He handed his bowl to Akumalik and patted her hand as it met his. She smiled at him.

"Thank you," was all she said but there was an intimacy and an allusion that spoke volumes to him and restored immediately his sense of wellbeing. It was short lived.

"I think you had better deal with this. My Inuktitut isn't good enough."

Alistair had returned to the kitchen, suppressed amusement evident in his body language if not actually on his face. "But I did pick up the fact that the shaman was needed."

Sandy stormed to the door and there was much noise as he took the group into the Eskimo room. He was back within a few minutes after the native group had shuffled disconsolately out of the house. Akumalik and Alistair waited expectantly for an explanation. Reluctantly and with obvious discomfort Sandy obliged them.

"They wanted me to visit Irvana. She has been with Tupilliqqut for three years now and still has not conceived a child. They thought I could go into a trance, summon up my spirits and then fly to the moon to bring back a baby for her," he mumbled and then seeing Alistair double up with laughter, roared "I gave them 'fly to the moon'! I'm far too busy I told them. Go to the other shaman. He's got more time on his hands for trips to the moon."

By now Alistair was uncontrollable and even Akumalik, not quite understanding the joke but infected by Alistair's laughter had joined in the mirth. At last Sandy, appreciating the absurdity of the situation, chuckled with them. Gasping for breath, Alistair sank on to a chair.

"You know what that means of course," he offered eventually. "You get to sleep with Irvana in payment of your shaman's fee. And after that episode there is every possibility that the moon baby will arrive in nine month's time. She's a nice-looking girl. I would have thought a great magician like you would have been only too happy to help out. I wonder if, as the sorcerer's apprentice, I could volunteer," he concluded wistfully.

"I've enough on my hands," Sandy said with satisfaction. "Talking of which we've wasted enough time this morning on foolishness. There'll be queues outside the store. Get out and get trading."

Left alone, Akumalik and Sandy looked at each other.

"I assume you don't want me flying off to the moon on Irvana's behalf?" he teased. She shook her head.

"And not on my behalf either," she replied seriously. "After Martee the shaman told me I could have no more children. So even you could not intercede for me. I hope you will not be disappointed that I will bear no child?"

He studied her, initially with disbelief but quickly reshuffled his thoughts to accept and understand her thinking. She too believed he had magic powers, that what he had done yesterday made him mystical and potent. She had lived all her life with these beliefs, why should she suddenly change because she had lived a short time with the white man? She had laughed with him and Alistair but in ignorance of the real reason for their mirth. Ah well, he concluded, he had no intention of changing her convictions. It was part of her heritage and after all the whole of the Christian faith was based on one man rising from the dead. Admittedly his priests didn't go flying off to the moon to collect babies for infertile females but there was no harm in her faith. And it was a certain relief to him that she would not become pregnant. He was too old for fatherhood now and he wanted their relationship to remain discreet. He knew there would be no stigma attached to either of them if their secret became known but he was a private man and he felt that she too preferred to keep their intimacy theirs alone.

"You are a good woman," he told her simply. "You are all I need."

CHAPTER 34

The war had taken its toll of the Richardson family. Ella's father had not been called into the armed forces, to the family's immense relief. But, in London on business, he had been one of the dozens of unlucky victims of Hitler's bombardment of the capital and his stunned wife and daughters had brought back his body for a Scottish burial. Mrs. Richardson had then thrown herself into the war effort with punishing vigour, spending exhausting hours at the hospitals, driving herself in an attempt to block out her grief. In her weakened state she had been an early casualty of a flu epidemic and Ella found herself alone and heartbroken in the large house in Carnoustie, her sister Florence having moved, with her new husband, to their own cottage.

Ella herself had been stricken by the flu at the same time as her mother. She had pulled through but her illness had necessitated rigorous medical checks that revealed, to her horror and dread, traces of tuberculosis in her lungs. She was initially panic-stricken and she felt the eerie certainty that she had brought this disease upon herself. Hadn't she intimated to Sandy that she had a life-threatening illness that prevented her from joining him? It had been, of course, a face-saving ruse that at the time she had not thought twice about fabricating. *It serves you right, you wished it upon yourself* – the phrases pounded in her brain and, combined with the terror of the dreadful threat itself, and with the added grief over her parents' deaths coming so quickly behind each other, she retreated into herself, becoming a neurotic recluse on the border of insanity. Florence tried to help but her very happiness with Henry, her loving and attentive husband, served only to contrast with Ella's own bleak existence.

Sandy's letters, at the best infrequent and always impersonal, had, during the war years, trickled almost to a standstill. And then, in 1944, with positive rumours about the war ending lifting the lives of everyone, she received a long and happy letter from him. It was curiously unlike the others. There was more of him in it, she could almost hear his voice telling his news. It was still all about the monotony, as far as she could understand it, of dealing with furs and weather and those peculiar natives of whom he seemed so fond, but there was something upbeat and different; as though there was a new influence in his life, as though he was seeing things through different eyes. And he had enclosed a photograph. There was a group of three standing beside a bank of snow which towered above their heads and which concealed, so he explained on the back, his house. Until the snow could be moved, he elaborated further in his letter, they had to tunnel through to the door and there was every possibility that even when they had cleared the snow another blizzard would deposit a thicker blanket of snow over them. Still, he added cheerfully, it kept them warm, both the digging and clearing involved and in the meantime there was the extra insulation that the overcoat of snow gave to the house. It sounded tedious and an infuriating nuisance to Ella.

The clerk Alistair looked a friendly young man, she thought, and then there was the housekeeper Akomulik, who she had not heard of before. Sandy had been full of praise for her in the letter. Wonderful stews, excellent bread and porridge and she coped with everything, unexpected visitors, medical disasters, the occasional household calamity, with a quiet fortitude that calmed everyone. A virtual paragon, sniffed Ella. What was it about these people that Sandy found so attractive? She could see nothing that was appealing in the round smiling faces, the high cheekbones, the compact little bodies bundled into furs. But it was the image of Sandy that she studied so intently and so often. Only his face was really visible. The rest of him, like the others, was trussed up in animal skins, a furry hood around his head and shaggy gloves and boots on his hands and feet. But

Aupaluktuk - the Red One

his eyes still twinkled with that grin that still could turn her insides to water as he squinted at the camera in the sparkling sunlight reflected off the snow. He never aged, she thought enviously. Of course it was only an amateur photograph. Perhaps there would be the tell-tale lines chiselling their ominous marks into his face if only she could see him face to face. And a surge of longing to see him, to be with him, to touch him and talk to him and have him make her life worth living again shook her with such a force that it brought on a violent bout of coughing that left her weak and frightened.

She could not get him out of her mind. There was little enough to occupy it apart from the intermittent worry about the behaviour of the servants and her frustration at her inability to dismiss anyone knowing she would not be able to replace them. Money was not a problem. Her father had invested carefully and well and she was amply provided for but nowadays no one wanted to do domestic work. There were too many well-paid jobs in the factories with little responsibility, as far as she could judge, and even less demand for loyalty and commitment. Ardmore was a big house that needed experienced staff to run it efficiently. She found daily she had to overlook deficiencies in attitude and performance in order to preserve the status quo. And she needed people. Everyone she loved had deserted her: Father, Mother, Florence and of course Sandy. Sandy, who had promised so much and then let her down, betrayed her for a cold impossible country peopled by inarticulate savages.

She would go mad if she stayed here alone. She forced herself off her bed and grimly faced the mirror. Initially she saw a middle-aged woman dressed in drab but expensive clothes, an expression of unbending distaste now challenged by a powerful self-pity, on her face. She almost turned away but then she made herself stare at her own reflection and slowly she saw another self. The T.B. had affected her weight. Now the fleshy jowls had tightened around her chin and she could see bone structure that she had never guessed she possessed. The illness brightened and enlarged her eyes and her skin was flushed with a contained fever. She looked … interesting. She thought of pale consumptive heroines, Mary Shelley types, with adoring suitors at their feet. It was ironic. She had a terrifying, death-threatening illness and yet, if she smiled – she forced her lips into a faint indication of pleasure – she looked better, more alluring than she had ever looked.

The doctor had suggested Switzerland once the war was over and travel was easier of course. The fresh mountain air, the cold, would do wonders for her, could effect a cure. She had dismissed the recommendation out of hand. She knew no one in Switzerland, she would be lonely. The germ of an idea started to form and with it her excitement grew and her heart pounded. There was somewhere she could go where the air was pure, cold, clinically cold. Where she would be looked after and cherished by the one person she wanted to be with. She would go to Sandy, take her place at last by his side. The combination of the restorative weather and the contentment she would undoubtedly find in his company would save her. She would be cured. She could face the austerity, she knew she could. After all, what sort of life was she living alone in luxury in this house surrounded by possessions for which she had no use. He would, he must welcome this new woman back into his life. Her decision now made, she began to work for its success.

She walked to the writing bureau in her bedroom and pulled out a page of thick expensive vellum embossed with her address. She directed her first letter to the managers of the Arctic Division, Hudson's Bay Company, Winnipeg. She kept it short and to the point. She intended, as soon as arrangements could be made – there was an implication here that she expected immediate action – to join her husband, Alexander Lunan at his post at Baker Lake. He would be writing to them to confirm this. In the meantime she would be grateful if they could acquaint her of the soonest available shipping times. She appreciated the havoc that the war had caused to sea passage but she was willing to travel by any transport they thought appropriate. They would realize, she was sure, that she was anxious to join her husband at the earliest opportunity. She thanked them for their anticipated assistance and remained, sincerely, E. Lunan (Mrs.)

She re-read it with satisfaction and then started the more difficult letter to Sandy. She had half a dozen false starts and then opted again to keep it short, advising him of a decision made rather than posing a request to him. She told him that the war and the misfortunes it had visited upon her had changed her attitude to life. She knew now that her place was by his side wherever that might be and that by writing to Head Office she had already put into motion the necessary machinery to bring this about as soon as possible. She was confident that all this would meet with his approval and she looked forward with anticipation to his early, positive reply. She thanked him, in a postscript, for his recent letter and photograph. She was, she assured him, excited about meeting both Alistair and the housekeeper and was particularly looking forward to teaching the Eskimo woman some favourite Scottish recipes that would improve and vary their seemingly never-ending diet of stew.

She was pleased with her efforts. There was no need to mention her illness. Sandy knew she had been bluffing when she had manufactured the disease as a reason to remain in Scotland. Now it was a reality but, for the time being, it would stay her secret. She would tell him, of course, when they were together and together they would conquer it. She had only to wait impatiently for the wheels of bureaucracy to turn but at last she had a future ahead of her, something to look forward to. She kept her plans to herself but the improvement in her mood and attitude was noticed with relief by the servants and her sister. Long may it continue, they all thought privately, and only Florence wondered what had caused it.

CHAPTER 35

The Christmas celebrations at Baker Lake in 1944 were particularly joyful. The Allies were going to win the war! The European offensive had taken place in the summer and although progress was patchy the outcome was now no longer in doubt. Another war to end all wars was drawing to its close leaving the world shaken, impoverished and in mourning for its millions of dead but with the unshaken conviction that right had triumphed once more and that God had awarded the winner's laurels to His chosen people.

Privately, Sandy felt things were not quite as black and white as most preferred to believe. His view of war was jaundiced forever by his experiences and knowledge of the Great War. He believed passionately that democracy had to be defended and upheld against the wicked prejudices and totalitarianism of fascism but he was not so sure that all the troops of the righteous were indeed clothed in shining armour or that the allies of today would prove to be the most suitable of bedfellows. But, for the most part, he kept his own counsel and only occasionally shared his unformed but insistent fears with Akumulik. She listened and soothed. It was all she could do. She did not fully understand his misgivings, only that he had them and that they troubled him. Her world, her horizon was so narrow, she knew that, but probably because of that she was happy. And when she indicated her happiness to him he too became happy. It was so simple.

And then suddenly it was not so simple after all. Early January Sandy sat down as usual to listen to the radio. During the endless night of winter it always seemed particularly important to him to stay in touch with the outside world. It was mostly insignificant chit-chat. Robbie reminding Art that he hadn't forgotten the wager they had on the outcome of the Toronto Maple Leafs and the Montreal Canadiens match; Pete congratulating Hank on becoming the father of a daughter at last after four strapping sons; endless questions about the weather, advisability of travel, reports of minor injuries and the success or otherwise of suggested remedies. But officialdom used it too and Sandy unconsciously straightened his posture as though coming to attention when he heard his name mentioned by Pete Nichols, his area manager in Winnipeg. Over the years they had become firm friends, respecting each other's opinions even when in disagreement. There was a certain amount of hesitation in the senior man's voice, discernible even over the crackle of the airways.

"I've got a personal message for you here, Sandy. I'll be sending you the details as soon as we can get mail up to you but thought I'd better get your initial reaction as soon as possible. Is it all right for me to continue?"

Thoroughly alarmed now but pretty sure he was not about to be informed of a death or obvious disaster, Sandy clenched his fists and grunted tersely an affirmative.

"O.K." Pete cleared his throat and took a deep breath. "We've had a communication from your wife – there's a letter here for you from her too, probably about the same matter. She says she's decided to join you at Baker Lake and could we make the appropriate arrangements. I hadn't heard anything from you about the matter so thought I'd better clear it with you before continuing..."

There was a staggering silence from Sandy so Pete continued uneasily. "I had understood that Mrs. Lunan had a medical condition that prevented her from living in the Arctic" – a slight pause while he waited hopefully for some response and then carried on nervously – "but I guess it must have cleared up? Good news eh?" Still nothing and now the silence was deafening. Eager to be finished with the message and unnerved by Sandy's lack of response he babbled on, "Well that's settled then. She'll have to have a medical of course. The company doctor in Edinburgh will see to it. We'll set it all up. Any questions, you know I'll be only too happy to answer."

Again a pause and then at last Sandy's voice on the radio. It was barely audible but it was brief. "Thanks Pete. I'll be in touch."

Sandy slumped back in his chair in shock. He put his hands over his eyes and sat for five minutes completely numb, thoughts chasing each other inconsequentially through his brain, unable to focus, a rising sense of panic fluttering in his chest and with the certainty that he was trapped like an animal awaiting its fate. Finally, with supreme will-power, he forced himself to be calm, to think logically, to find a solution. But there was none. Oh yes, he could refuse, point blank. Tell Winnipeg he did not want her here and they would respect his wishes without question. There would be speculation, of course, he would be the talk of the Northern Territories for a while but he could weather that and it would be a nine-day wonder as it had been when she had left him at Port Harrison. But then he had been blameless. The decision had been hers alone and he had respected it, with relief admittedly but that did not alter the fact that he had done his best by her.

Now she had changed her mind, for what reasons he had no idea. He did not understand her. He could speculate until the cows came home and still he would be no closer to the truth, but he was pretty sure of one thing. It had nothing to do with a long-delayed desire on her part to make his life more pleasant. Whatever her reasons, he was obliged to accede. They were still married, she had rights and it was his duty to fulfil his responsibilities, however inadvisable or abhorrent they seemed to him. He would have to tell Akumulik.

He did so that night. Although instinctively he would have preferred to delay the telling indefinitely on the stupid premise that if people did not know perhaps it would not happen, he knew it was essential that he was honest with her. She was so touchingly open herself. And although there were disagreements, rows even, between them, nothing festered below the surface because it remained unsaid. He knew he would be bad-tempered, probably for the foreseeable future, he realized with despair, and she was entitled to know why, long before the reason for his irritability appeared.

She was quiet at first, taking her time to reflect upon and digest this unexpected bombshell. And then she began to ask questions, reasonable ones, ones he had asked himself and to which he could find no answers. Why had this wife of Sandy's suddenly decided to leave Scotland, at her age – a factor Sandy had not thought of – to come to Sandy when she had not wanted him before? He did not know and after all it was not an issue. She was coming, that was that. They would have to accept it. Would he tell his wife about their relationship? No! It was not possible, replied Sandy with alacrity, although privately he admitted that would certainly solve his problem. They would not see a hair of Ella's head if she even suspected such a situation. Would she, Akumulik, still be needed as housekeeper when this wife of Sandy's came to look after him? Of course, he told her, pulling her closer to him in his arms, of course. She was very dear to him, he wanted her to stay, but they would have to accept that they could no longer be like this.

She nodded. This was how it must be. Inwardly she cried. She did not want to lose this man for whom she had such love and tenderness. She had been willing to share him with this Scottish woman but even that was not to be. It must be sufficient for her that she could stay near him and look after him. She did not know how easy it would be for her to serve the wife but she must learn. This is how it must be she repeated to herself.

Ella felt she could share her secret with her sister when she heard from the Hudson's Bay Company that a medical had been arranged for her in Edinburgh. It was springtime and she felt a corresponding surge of hope and optimism as she faced the new year and her new future. Florence looked at her with astonishment and horror.

"But Ella, why?" was all she could say.

"Why? Why?" Ella snapped, her voice rising with irritation at the reception her news had generated. Suddenly everything soured. She had been sure her sister would be delighted for her and that together they would plan for her departure as they had done for her wedding all those years ago.

"Because there's nothing left for me here. Because he's my husband and it is time he took up his responsibilities in a practical sense at last. Because I've waited long enough for him here, in vain it appears, so I must go to him."

She glared at Florence, daring her to object. Florence decided she had to speak her mind. She wished Henry was by her side to help her face her sister who, from high good humour, was now definitely in one of her moods. Henry always told her Ella reduced her to a timorous little mouse and that she must stand up for herself. She ventured a nervous response.

"Are you sure it's for the best?" She addressed her remarks to a spot behind Ella's head, refusing to look in her eyes and be further intimidated by the fury she felt must be flashing from them. "There's your ... condition." The last word was spoken tentatively. No one openly acknowledged that Ella was consumptive. It was somehow not quite nice. "You know how down you were after mother's death. Is it wise to go so far from reliable medical advice?" And quickly, before she could be interrupted and before she lost her courage, "Has Sandy agreed to this? He's probably set in his ways by now. It could be difficult for you both to adjust."

"How dare you suggest my own husband will not want me! How dare you!" Incoherent with anger, Ella searched for words to express her outrage. "Do you think the Company would have authorized my journey without his approval? Even someone as lacking in sense and sensibility as you appear to be must realize he has agreed. Not only agreed but rejoiced," she lied.

She had not, in fact, heard from him directly but had received an agreement to proceed via the Company. "And I am better than I have ever been. Look at me, just look at me!" she shrieked. And she did indeed look splendid in her passion, her gaunt face flushed and her eyes burning. Florence shrank back from the onslaught and then as quickly rushed forward to catch her sister. Exhausted by her rage, Ella collapsed suddenly in a paroxysm of coughing which racked her shrunken frame and left her sobbing for breath. Both women gazed in fascinated terror at the fresh blood that stained the linen handkerchief that Ella took away from her mouth.

CHAPTER 36

The result of the medical was a shock to no one. Ella went through the motions of the examination but she knew, and at last admitted, that not only could she never travel to Baker Lake but her illness was incurable and her life expectancy short. There was no point in notifying Sandy, the Company would do that with expressions of regret. There was no point in anything at all, she determined, no point in anger or regret or recrimination. She lapsed into a sickly existence, rarely leaving her room, admitting few visitors apart from her sister and brother-in-law, leaving the few remaining servants to run the house as best they could, demanding nothing of anyone except her simple meals and a basic standard of cleanliness.

Florence was at first alarmed and distressed at the change in Ella. It was a relief that she no longer had to face Ella's mood swings and temper outbursts but she recognized that with this switch in temperament, Ella had lost interest in her life. No amount of cajoling or nagging or deliberately attempting to provoke moved her and eventually Florence accepted the inevitable. Ella had decided to die. Even the letter that arrived from Sandy full of sympathy and, Florence was sure, simulated regret, failed to generate even a spark of interest from her sister.

Sandy received the news with such a mixture of emotions that it took him days before he was able to acknowledge even to himself that his unconscious prayers had been answered. He was genuinely shocked that Ella's illness was as grave as had been indicated. A man of robust health himself, he had a terror and dislike that bordered on the phobic of illness and the insidious symptoms of T.B. filled him with loathing. He was racked with pity for Ella and with an inexplicable guilt that somehow he was to blame for her predicament. If he had cared more, if he had been with her, if he had not wanted so badly for her to be prevented from joining him at Baker Lake. He felt he had wished this dreadful disease upon her.

But his prevailing emotion was one of relief. It was as though the dark Arctic days of winter had suddenly and unseasonably become a gleaming glistening summer. He debated with himself how to tell Akumulik. In the end he kept it simple. Ella was no longer coming, she was sick and had to stay in her country where the doctors would fight to save her life. And if they did, queried Akumulik, will she come when she is better? She will never be strong enough to travel, she will never come here now. Will you leave to go to her? The question Sandy was dreading even asking himself had to be faced and answered. No, he said, hesitating at first and then speaking with conviction: No. I'm needed here, the Company needs me, the people need me. There are many people in her country who will look after my wife, her sister, the servants, (he faltered), her friends, and we have become strangers after all these years apart. She would find no solace in my presence, he concluded.

At last Akumulik beamed. Her face lit up with happiness. There was no need for more questions. Sandy had told her the important things. She could sense his struggle with his thoughts and she knew his decision to stay would torment him for many days yet but quizzing him about his feelings would not help. Only the resumption of routine, hard work and hard conditions and, above all, the passage of time would calm him. And she would be there to comfort him.

He was due home leave at this time but, unable to face the situation with Ella, secretly terrified he would be emotionally blackmailed to stay if he returned to Scotland, he opted instead for a short break in Winnipeg. Even that he was reluctant to take, preferring the isolation of Baker Lake to any of the dubious pleasures of civilization. But Company policy demanded a break and a medical and so he went. His brief meeting with the head office management prompted the following memo, a copy of which was sent to him and provided him with wry amusement:

Management interview with Alexander Lunan
Discussion Memo – 28th August, 1945

Having in mind A. Lunan's statement of several years ago that he intended to finish out his period of service (until next furlough due) at Baker Lake, and then retire, I discussed the matter with him and found that he had the following in mind.

1. He has been, and for the past several years, estranged from his wife and his original desire to resign for the purpose of joining her in Scotland no longer holds. (She has continually refused to come out to Canada to join him, until the winter of 1944/45 when she asked that arrangements be made for her to join her husband. With Lunan's consent we made preliminary arrangements only to find that her health did not permit her to go to an isolated post. On that account arrangements for her transportation were cancelled on authority from Lunan).

2. It is his desire to put in three more years at Baker Lake then, when his next furlough is due, proceed to the old country on holiday.

3. I pointed out the possibility of his being transferred to another post during the course of the three years. He stated that he would prefer to quit rather than take a transfer at this stage. He stated, however, that if and when he completed his three-year term at Baker Lake and his vacation, he would be quite willing to take charge of any Eskimo post at which the Company would wish to place him.

4. To understand Lunan's ideas it is also necessary to understand his background. He has had many years in the North, first with Revillion Freres and later with the Hudson's Bay Company. A large proportion of this time he has been alone. He is very methodical and on that account has acquired fixed habits and ideas to a greater extent than would the average individual living under the same conditions. (As a case in point, he had made up his mind that he would not have a medical – he said he felt fine and didn't need a doctor to tell him there was nothing wrong with him. A great deal of persuasion was necessary before he finally consented to the medical. He was found to be in first-class condition).

Aupaluktuk - the Red One

5. Lunan is an exceptionally good man on the job, well liked by the Eskimos, speaks their language fluently, and keeps his post in splendid condition at all times.

6. All in all I would classify him as the best Eskimo Post Manager in the section – comparable to Angus Gavin as a trader, but better than Gavin insofar as the physical aspect of the post operation is concerned.

(WEB/DFL WINNIPEG 31 August 1945)

"Fixed habits indeed!" thought Sandy with indignation. If they meant by that "routine", then fair enough. Routine was essential in even the most civilized of lives but in the conditions in which he lived it was more than essential, it was the difference between life and death, for him and those who depended upon him. However, all in all, the report was fair although he had no recollection of ever voicing his intention to join his wife in Scotland. Probably blurted out at a time when he was being questioned too intimately about the state of his marriage. They valued him, that was clear, and he was fairly certain, by the tenor of the memo, that he had at least three more years at Baker Lake.

It had, in fact, proved to be a useful trip to Winnipeg. Nothing had gone wrong in his absence and by the warmth of their greeting on his return it was obvious he had been missed by all at the post and by Akumulik in particular. Naturally he brushed off any attempt to show affection with a brusque "Aye, it's just as well I'm back. Looks like the place has gone to rack and ruin." But he enjoyed their welcome and sat up that night beyond his ten o'clock bedtime, telling with skill and humour of the joshing he had given the unfortunate doctor assigned to give him his medical. And later, in bed with Akumulik, he felt a sense of joy and well-being, a rare moment of perfect pleasure. "I'm the luckiest man in the world," he murmured quietly to himself.

CHAPTER 37

The recent war had left the Canadian government with a few unanswered questions. Invasion from the north – it had not happened but it could have. How vulnerable were they, would men and machinery survive any sort of attack in the Arctic wastes? Exercise Musk Ox set out to probe and test.

Labelled a "scientific journey of exploration", it was definitely, as far as Sandy was concerned, a military exercise to paper over glaring gaps in national defence and he was to be part of the initial stages of the operation.

Preparation began three weeks ahead of the main expedition. While the men, forty-seven of them with eleven snowmobiles and one amphibious weasel, began a six week training programme in Churchill, bulldozers covered 500 miles in three weeks to arrive at Baker Lake to clear and lengthen the runway before the supply planes and caches of fuel and spare parts began to arrive.

It was heady stuff being part of a military operation again. They had missed the war in essence at Baker Lake but this vital exercise gave them a sense of the urgency and precise planning needed in wartime conditions without the danger. Sandy had been told of Musk Ox's objectives by its leader Lt. Col. P.D. Baird. Number one was to study the co-operation between the military and the air force and to work out methods of air supply. Number two was to test the mobility of the snowmobiles in territory never before covered by motor vehicles. And finally, the scientific objectives, important as they were but very much a smoke screen to hide the military nature of the operation; to record magnetic variations, to make astronomic observations, to study the effects of the Aurora Borealis, to correct existing maps and to cope with the ever present problems of weather.

The arrival of the main body of the exercise was exciting and busy. Sandy was in his element, logistics a natural talent of his and with typical efficiency he had everyone boarded out either in his own house, the missions or the R.C.M.P. station. The soldiers had brought tents with them but were visibly gratified when shown to more substantial accommodation. They had brought their own supplies of food but again Akumalik's caribou stew was a welcome change from their own canned and dried victuals. They were an entertaining crew, explaining the course of the journey so far, from Churchill to Eskimo Point and from there to Baker Lake. Uncomfortable travel along the rough sea ice of the Hudson Bay but so far, touch wood, no problems that couldn't be dealt with.

"Aye, you've got it all ahead of you no doubt," Sandy observed gloomily. "Your route overland to the Perry River and Coppermine, quite a challenge. I doubt any white man has travelled that territory before. You'll be praying for clement weather and when that fails, as it will do, you'll be grateful for the help of any Inuit wintering in that area. Think of them as your good luck charm. They've saved more lives than I'd care to recount."

The men had smiled amongst themselves, privately categorising Sandy as a dour Scot with doom and gloom on the brain but in no time at all they were hailing him as a "fine guy" when his stories had them weak with laughter and the rum bottle was passed again around the table.

And the next morning the weather struck. Winds that had howled with deafening fury, snow that blinded and stung and cut any exposed skin. They went about their tasks of maintenance and thorough cleaning of all vehicles with difficulty but the reality of February in the Barrens was suddenly grim and frightening and the old Scot's warning was now ever-present in their minds.

It was an anticlimax when they left. The adrenaline-rush of organising, feeding, helping with the machines, socialising, left the Baker Lake community with a sense of unaccustomed idleness when they were alone again. Tempers frayed and silences grew longer. But it was temporary. And very soon each of them became grateful again for their isolation and wondered how they could have thought to enjoy such disruption to the well-ordered rhythm of their lives.

There was a gratifying postscript to the part they played in Exercise Musk Ox in the form of a letter copied to Sandy from Headquarters.

ROYAL CANADIAN AIR FORCE
Rockcliffe, Ontario
20th March, 1946

Mr. R. H. Chesshire,
General Manager Northern Posts,
Fur Trade Department,
Hudson's Bay Company,
WINNIPEG, Manitoba.

Dear Mr. Chesshire,

As you are probably well aware, there has been recently a very considerable amount of joint R.C.A.F -Army activity in the Hudson Bay area in connection with Exercise "Musk-Ox".

I have just recently returned from visiting the Exercise, after inspecting the R.C.A.F. Detachment there which is a part of No. 9 (Transport) Group. During this time I visited Baker Lake and met your Post Manager, Mr. A. Lunan.

Mr. Lunan at Baker Lake has suffered practically a full scale invasion, as this has been a prominent staging point for the Exercise, but he has accepted the situation with the utmost of grace. The R.C.A.F. "Musk-Ox" men have the highest praise for the assistance and co-operation Mr.

Lunan has extended. He has left them with an indelible impression of the good will and efficiency of the Hudson's Bay Company.

In past years I have travelled considerably in Northern Canada and have met many Hudson's Bay Post Managers, and on this trip it was warming indeed to meet again the traditional hospitality of the Hudson's Bay Company. Mr. Lunan most impressively upholds the best of your Company's reputation.

I would like to express to you on behalf of the R.C.A.F., our sincere thanks for the assistance rendered by Mr. Lunan to the personnel of Operation "Musk-Ox". It has been very exceptional, even in consideration of the high standards of your Company elsewhere.

Yours very sincerely,
(L. E. Wray) Air Commodore
A.O.C., No. 9 (Transport) Group
Rockcliffe, Ontario.

Sandy read the commendation with a satisfied smile. "I should think so," he muttered with fake disgust. "Had to go on half liquor rations after that greedy bunch swept through."

CHAPTER   38

The winter of 1946 was vicious and unrelenting. The supply ship M.K. Neophyte came in October and despite their frantic efforts to unload and load in record time, the freeze set in and the ship and its crew were imprisoned until the thaw began in June the following year. Extra supplies for them had to be flown in regularly from Chesterfield Inlet but again the blizzards sought to disrupt and every journey was fraught with danger. Day followed anxious day in a frightening world of screaming white fury. More and more Inuit fought their way back to the Lake to build their igloos by the trading post in the hope that the Company would save them from starvation or death from the unrelenting cold. And Sandy hated their growing dependence upon him and his supplies. He knew, throughout their history, that the Inuit had met and dealt with conditions like this. Indeed there had been casualties. He had only to look at Akumalik and remember the circumstances of her girlhood to feel the awfulness of such a fate. But there was a nagging feeling within him that somehow, he and his life saving shopful of supplies were destroying the natural order of things.

There was more to brood and dwell upon in February 1947, with the news that Ella had succumbed to tuberculosis and died in Ashludie Hospital in Monefieth. He spent days in silence, trapped in his own thoughts of guilt, regret and finally relief. He had agonised, in one way or another, over Ella for as long as he had known her and now, at last, there was no longer any need to. He wondered briefly what life would have been like if she had stepped off the boat with him all those many years ago. He would have liked to have had children; would she have provided them? It was too difficult to imagine. All he could recollect was her pale face twisted with disappointment and rage as she screamed at him, "I will not go with you!" and he was left to go ashore alone.

There was a meaningful crash as Akumalik clattered a mug of tea down on the table in from of him. She stared at him, hands on her hips and without saying anything turned away from him and stalked back to the kitchen, her back stiff with disapproval. And that was the full stop to his silent introspection. She had waited patiently and with tact while he withdrew from them all to deliberate and struggle with himself over Ella's death. But now it was enough, she was telling him. Time to get on with living, with laughing and with loving her. My god, she was a wonderful woman, Sandy thought with immense satisfaction.

He returned to Scotland the following year for a three-month vacation, most of it spent in Edinburgh. He paid a brief visit to Carnoustie to visit Florence and her family who had, it now appeared, inherited all of Ella's possessions, including the house, leaving no one in any doubt of what she had thought of her absentee husband. Any fond thoughts Sandy may have had at being left a wealthy widower were swiftly dispelled. It had all the prospects of being an awkward meeting but in fact there was no animosity from her sister – just a sadness that Ella had led such a wasted life of bitterness and pride. She even offered, with her husband's approval, a settlement on Sandy,, embarrassed as she was to inherit what she thought should be legally his. But he declined with thanks. He had all he needed, he told them. His needs were few and were more than met with his salary from the Company and the spartan life he led in the Arctic. "I'm completely content," he stated and as he spoke those words he realised how wonderfully true they were.

It was a good leave. All the embarrassment with Ella on previous visits was now behind him and he could enjoy his own country, his old haunts, his friendship with Dom, with an easy familiarity which gave him great pleasure. He stayed in Edinburgh with Aggie and his niece Janet. Aggie had returned from Canada on Bill's death and for the education of the children.

Billie, Janet's younger brother, had met a sudden and shocking end when, training to become a pilot at the beginning of the war, his plane had crashed and snuffed out his young life. The two women were devastated and there were evenings of maudlin remembrance which Sandy suffered gladly, knowing that talking about Billie helped them to bear their pain.

But mostly they doted on him and revelled in the company of a man about the house again, especially one as interesting and charming as Sandy. He became the focal point of many a dinner party, Aggie proud of her now not-so-young brother and his fascinating life. It made Sandy think seriously about his approaching retirement which, in six years time when he was 60, was the norm in Arctic outposts. It would be a wrench, no doubt about that, but with his savings he would be comfortably well-off and life in Edinburgh with two adoring females and a ready made social life could be most acceptable. He deliberately blocked off the thought of Akumalik. It was still too far away. He would think of something, but not just yet.

150

CHAPTER 39

But in the blink of an eye it was time to think of it. The years
flew by. Alistair was replaced by Ed Spracklin and he in turn by
the new clerk Eric Mitchell, a young Scot from Murrayshire
who was sent to Baker Lake as a first posting. It had been an
inauspicious beginning for the two. Sandy had thought he was
getting another man, Joe Gleeson, who had been a clerk at
Chesterfield Inlet and who had not impressed Sandy at all, probably due to his devout Catholicism. Unfair? Undoubtedly, but
he was unwilling and therefore unable to alter his prejudices at
his age. So when Eric arrived at Churchill to await the first
available flight to Baker Lake, there was a strong reluctance on
the part of the pilot, Commander Black, to take him. One
excuse after another kept Eric kicking his heels around the air
base for five days until it dawned on everyone that he was not
the bete noir that Sandy was so anxious to keep from his station.

It worked in his favour after that with Sandy so eager to
compensate for the misunderstanding that he was hospitality
itself when Eric eventually arrived. He learned from Akumalik
later that he had even sat in Sandy's chair and not a word of
complaint was uttered. Humble pie indeed! What did make
the pair of them laugh was Joe's eventual posting to Baker Lake,
not with the Hudson's Bay Company but with a meteorological
team to do tests on the ionosphere. And even that had its com-
pensations as Joe had married Joyce, who had a nursing degree
and she was able to help with the first aid and medical supplies.
There were still a large proportion of the Inuit however who
insisted upon treatment from Sandy whose "shaman" status
was still legendary! And that in turn kept the missionaries from

his door as they tried in vain to convince the Inuit that it was their God who healed and saved, not some powerful spirit lodged in the body of Mr. Alexander Lunan.

The station was becoming busier now with visitors from all walks of life. Now an air service was operating on a regular basis the intellectuals, the scientists, the botanists and even a few adventurous writers and photographers started to come. Although unfailingly hospitable, Sandy's generous nature could be tested if weather conditions forced an extended stay and he usually sent guests who had overstayed their welcome off to the Catholic mission – "for a change of scenery," he would say persuasively. He made an exception with Richard Harrington, the famous photographer who was responsible for the book *Face of the Arctic*, and the two spent hour after hour in conversation, enlivening the long Arctic nights with their stories and reminiscences. Sandy thrived on stimulating talk and Akumalik found him happier and more talkative with everyone after such visits. She had learned to live with his ups and downs and now gave as good as she got when his temper frayed and he criticised unfairly.

She thought with satisfaction and a touch of remorse of the day she had cut, by accident, one of the fish lines that sank. It was no major disaster but you would have thought the world had come to an end the way Sandy ranted and raved at her for her stupidity. "It's taken Eric and me all bloody day to retrieve the thing! Can't you watch what you're doing? D'you think we've nothing better to do than sit about freezing to death out there just because you didn't take your time and bring it in slowly?" On and on he went and she took it stoically, apologising at first and then lapsing into silence as he renewed his verbal attack. But gradually, throughout the day, she felt her own temper begin to rise. Enough was enough. She had said she was sorry, it had been an accident and she had taken the blame. She would not listen to any more of his abuse.

She was on her way out of the house with a bucket full of ash from the stove when he started again. Something snapped and she swung the bucket over her head and emptied its contents over him, catching him a nasty blow on the forehead as she did so. They both stared at each other in astonishment. Then the sight of him covered in ash with a trickle of blood running from the wound down his face, his mouth open with the shock started her laughing, laughing so hard that the tears came and her stomach ached with mirth. Unable to help himself, Eric too shook with unstoppable laughter and at last Sandy saw the ridiculousness of the situation.

"Well, I suppose I asked for that," he mumbled. "Just deserts. But you try that again, woman, and I'll not answer for the consequences. Now shut up the two of you and get me cleaned up and a bandage on this. I'll have a lump the size of an egg by tomorrow and it will take some explaining. And don't think you're going to tell everyone what really happened because I'll lie through my teeth and no one will believe you."

Later that night as they lay together Sandy had turned to her, his head still throbbing from the cut.

"You could have done me serious injury today, if that cut gets infected there could be complications."

She snuggled close to him and kissed the bandage. "You will be fine. And you know now that I am a woman of spirit. You think I could listen to talk like that and not act! Be careful in future not to upset me."

And Sandy lay awake for a long time wondering how he could tell her the thing that would upset her most. He was going to leave. His time with the Company had come to an end and he would have to leave her behind.

CHAPTER 40

In the end very little was said. Terrified there might be demonstrations of emotion during which there was every possibility that he might break down and, to his thinking, disgrace himself, Sandy pretended to himself that it was just a particularly long leave he was taking. Everyone knew otherwise of course, and there were the occasional embarrassed pauses when his "leave" was mentioned, until it became an unspoken agreement that, until the last moment, nothing should be said at all. Akumalik performed her duties mechanically, her mind numbed with anticipated pain, but although her nightly embraces with Sandy became more fierce and ardent she did not speak of her misery and they held each other with mutual love and understanding.

And then he was gone. Clenching his teeth to keep back the tears, he forced his mind to thoughts of the future. It would be a new start but with the comfortable buffer of old and familiar friends and scenery around him. He would be fine, the prospect was rosy.

It was a disaster. Aggie and Janet had left Edinburgh as Janet, now a newly-qualified doctor, had been offered a practise in Dunning, a small village about nine miles outside Perth. They had bought a pretty house, St. Andrews Cottage, with a fine and spacious garden and in no time they were an integral part of the small community. Janet quickly became a much admired and respected physician and Aggie, through work with the church and the Women's Guild, found herself in the position of matriarch, listened to with deference, her instructions acted upon without argument, her demands met without delay. It was a position she was born for.

But to Sandy it was a living death. He felt suffocated by the smallness of attitude and outlook. By the endless afternoons sitting with bone china cups of tea and dainty sandwiches listening politely as infinitesimal points of order were discussed in relation to a forthcoming fete or church bazaar. As snide remarks, heavily veiled as unctuous concern, were made about this person or that, in their absence of course, and self-preening matrons took obvious pleasure in the discomfort or misfortune of others. Puffed up with her new-found importance, Aggie not only frowned upon but came almost near to forbidding Sandy's infrequent visits to the local public house.

"We have our position to maintain you know, Sandy," was a phrase with which she seemed to preface every remark. And then: "It wouldn't do to mix with the locals, to become familiar. They look up to us and expect a certain standard of behaviour. Oh no, it won't do. It won't do at all." A pregnant silence while she waited, frowning at Sandy as he sulked in a corner of the overcrowded sitting room, for a response that would please her. Getting none, she continued: "I can't see the problem anyway. We have sherry and whisky here at the house, rum too if you really feel the need for it."

And he felt obliged, night after night, to sit in the stifling heat of the sitting room while Aggie sewed and Janet entertained them with stories of her day at the surgery. There were dinner parties but not with the educated and entertaining people he had met in Edinburgh. Now he sat with the local farm owners and their wives and discussion was all of grain prices, cattle feed, the latest in farm machinery. They listened with ill-concealed boredom when Sandy ventured an occasional story of his own but the subject of conversation quickly reverted to that which interested and affected their own narrow lives. He felt he was drowning slowly in a morass of small-minded gentility, of hypocrisy and affectation. He was beginning to dislike his sister with her new airs and graces and although he was inordinately fond of his niece and proud of her achievements, he needed more than a daily diet of her life in the surgery to keep him sane.

He thought he would move. Back to Edinburgh where he could buy a house or an apartment and take up the social life he had enjoyed on his leaves. He even made a trip to the capital to investigate the cost of such a venture but prices were prohibitive and places he could afford were not in the areas he could envisage would be suitable venues for the cosmopolitan dinner parties he had in mind. He became impatient and ill-tempered, upsetting Aggie when he spoke his mind and disrupting the hitherto pleasing calm of their days.

The solution to his misery came slowly, the drip-drip of an idea mulled over and examined, rejected and then resurrected. It was ridiculous, it was a defeat, they would laugh at him and say it was impossible, every possible reason for not doing what he knew he had to do battled with his desire to make it happen.

And to his amazement it did happen, with relative ease and with an end result he had never dared even to imagine. A phone call followed by a letter of request and within weeks he was re-employed as a trader for the Hudson's Bay Company! They were happy to have his services for another five years but then, at the mandatory retirement of sixty-five, he really would have to go. His posting: station manager at Baker Lake, a position they had not managed to fill since his departure and one they anticipated he would accept with pleasure.

He told Aggie and Janet of his decision and, stunned into silence at first, there followed much tut-tutting and shaking of heads, while doom-laden proverbs about the foolishness of turning back were trotted out with relish. However, seeing the change in him that just the prospect of returning to the Arctic had produced, they acknowledged it might be for the best after all.

"There's obviously still a lot of work inside of you, Sandy, you've still got things to do and apparently it's there that you do them best. Maybe when you come back to us again you'll be a more peaceful soul and will be able to settle better. But that God-forsaken place has a powerful pull on you, there's no denying that. Away with you, back to the fearful cold and your funny little native friends. We'll see you when you're finally ready, if that time ever comes, for civilisation."

He made it back to Baker Lake in time for the December issue of *The Moccasin Telegraph*, the Hudson's Bay Company monthly magazine, which made the following announcement:

ALEXANDER LUNAN   *(Retirement)*

During World War 1 he served with the Black Watch. In the early days of the war he was seconded to the Kings Own African Rifles and served throughout the German East African Campaign, terminating his war career as a Captain.

During his years of service at Baker Lake he had many interesting experiences. In 1929 when Baker Lake was the focal point in the search for the Colonel McAlpine party who were forced down on the Arctic Coast, Mr. Lunan's great experience was of valuable assistance. In 1931 Charles Lindberg visited. In more recent years Mr. Lunan came into contact with a large amount of traffic and visitors, and his tact and ability in coping with this type of work was of immeasurable importance to the company. Besides his reputation for friendliness and hospitality, visitors to the North will greatly miss him and his famous caribou stews.

Mr. Lunan plans on taking up residence in Scotland and hopes in the not-so-distant future to visit a brother who is presently living in Australia.

"Whose caribou stews?" was Akumalik's only comment when the article was read to her.

CHAPTER 41

She was not sure that his return had been for the best. She could not put words to the sadness she had felt when he left, the empty space in her life that not even the tenderness of her daughter and Nilak could fill. But she had known this would happen, known from the moment she acknowledged that she loved him that one day he would go, that he could not live out his life in this land of hers. She had coped silently with her loss and, as she knew it would, the pain had gradually dulled and the comforting sameness of her days helped her think again, with optimism, of her future.

And then he came back, a noisy, beaming, slightly abashed presence who filled the room with his pleasure and who informed them all repeatedly and with no semblance of credulity, "Don't think I'm back here because I missed you lot. Oh no! Here I was just settling down to enjoy a well-earned rest when a little bird tells me there's no one in charge here at Baker Lake. Not only that but the whole place is about to collapse, the station is ill-disciplined, people flapping about without direction like hooked fish." He shrugged delightedly. "What could I do? Someone has to sort you out, so here I am. I've got another five years to thrash you into shape. That should do it. Then perhaps I can leave you to do the job properly and not have the whole operation flounder the minute my back is turned."

He hugged her to him in front of them all and then, alarmed at this uncharacteristic demonstration of affection, turned her round, patted her behind and demanded a cup of tea. And it was all as it had been.

Except it was not the same. Their life was changing, their

isolation was threatened and small tragedies were played out around them monthly. Planes came in and brought infection and disease that the Inuit were powerless to resist. Influenza raged, adults and children died. The caribou came late and when they did many of the hunters were too sick to hunt. More and more nomadic families came to Baker Lake to build their igloos and pitch their tents around the station. Sandy hated their growing dependence upon the white man. He raved at the Government that garnered thousands of dollars in license fees from sportsmen who killed the caribou for sport alone and yet which failed to respond to the ever-increasing cries of desperation from the starving Inuit for food. He deplored the increasing influx of "experts" into the Barrens to look for mineral wealth, to conduct meteorological experiments, to wander curiously among the People, asking questions, making assumptions with little or no knowledge or understanding. He was almost apoplectic with rage when he read the words of a Mr. Lesage, Minister of the Department of Northern Affairs and National Resources, in a press release:

"As the tempo of activity steps up in Canada's far north there will be an increasing demand for skilled and semi-skilled labour. The supply of qualified white men who can endure life in the bleak and cold Arctic wastes is, however, extremely small. To the Eskimos, on the other hand, the hardships of the north form part of everyday life. In addition it is the opinion of many who have worked among them that they can be trained to meet the need for labour that is bound to arise. It is a common misconception that the Eskimo has the mentality of a child, but to those who know better he is a highly intelligent person who possesses many capabilities, most particularly an aptitude for all things mechanical. These natives of the north know no greater joy than driving a truck, running a boat, or caring for a machine..." *

"What in God's name are they trying to turn them into?" he bellowed in frustrated passion, "bloody tractor drivers? They are hunters, always have been and always should be if it weren't for the meddling of insensitive bureaucrats who seem hell-bent on shackling them to machines and knocking all their heritage and culture out of them. Haven't they done enough harm to

* Extract from *'THE DESPERATE PEOPLE'* by Farley Mowat

the Indian without now interfering and destroying the Inuit?"

It was, ironically, this same Department that bestowed upon him an honour as unexpected as it was gratifying. A copy of the letter sent to Peter Nichols was forwarded to Sandy in the summer of 1955.

Northern Administration DEPARTMENT
Office of the Director and Lands Branch,
Northern Affairs and National Resources
Ottawa, 10 June, 1955

Mr. P.A.C. Nichols,
Manager,
Arctic Division,
Hudson's Bay Company,
Winnipeg, Man.

Dear Pete,

You may be interested to know that at a meeting of the Canadian Board on Geographical Names, held on June 2, 1955, the name "LUNAN LAKE" was approved for the Wager Bay 56 SW and 56SE North-west Territories map sheet. This, of course, was named for Mr. Sandy Lunan of Baker Lake fame.

I understand that the present policy of the Board is to wait at least until individuals have retired before perpetuating their names. However, when the name "LUNAN" was put forward, it was considered an exceptional case.

I am advised that the lake in question is situated some ninety miles north-east of Baker Lake at approximately latitude 64 degrees 52 north and 93 degrees 05 west.

You may wish to pass this information on to Sandy.

Kindest regards,
Yours sincerely,,
(signed) J. Cantley

Sandy sat down heavily on his chair, momentarily at a loss for words, the letter dangling from his fingers.

"Well, who'd have believed it," he managed finally. "Fame at last!" A pause and then: "And not before time too."

CHAPTER 42

Sandy's disenchantment grew. He was obliged every year to submit a report to Headquarters about the running of the station and his 1956 report read: "*We have had quite a lot of sickness among the natives during the outfit – mostly colds and flu. Nearly every plane brought a fresh dose. Twenty-one natives died, eleven being children under one year old.*

"*The natives at this post depend entirely on caribou and fish for food other than white man's. No seal or walrus are available here. Caribou is getting scarcer every year so the outlook is that the native will have to live on fish and the white man's food, with the odd caribou thrown in. A lot more fish could be caught here but the natives are reluctant to setting nets – especially in the Back River area. I understand a government man is coming to teach and encourage them in this respect.*"

And again, in 1957: "*...the caribou hunt was an absolute failure last fall due to a change of migration route of the herd. Very few boots were bought due to a shortage of skins. We have had a good deal of sickness. An epidemic of measles, the first time here, broke out last fall and there were quite a few deaths.*

"*The new hospital has a new male nurse, G.M. Lang, a Scot from Ayrshire and a most excellent man. Married with one daughter. We had quite a number of visitors during the outfit, especially last summer. There were judicial men, mining inspectors, wild life men, Americans etc. but no one of any consequence.*"

Akumulik could see his frustration at what he believed was the destruction of his natives' way of life. They were becoming more reluctant to leave the supposed security of the post, they welcomed the advent of the family allowance that enabled them to buy milk for their children from the station, but they were losing their unique skills and adapting, with frightening speed to a life of idleness and lethargy. She saw too that he was unhappy at the steadily increasing development of the station. From an isolated outpost of fur traders, missionaries and police, Baker Lake now supported a weather station and a hospital, both staffed by men and their wives, swelling the numbers of the settlement from a mere seven white men in the 1930s to thirty-eight in 1956. A school was planned in the very near future to educate the growing numbers of children. More people, civilization, interference from government agencies.

But it was the increase in the Inuit population at the base that angered Sandy. Now there were almost 400 permanent residents and there was every indication that the number would continue to grow, despite his every effort to dissuade them.

His worst fears were realized when, after another failure of the caribou in 1958, the Inuit people throughout the Barrens were on the brink of starvation. The Department of Northern Affairs took drastic action and decreed that certain centres be set up where the Inuit should transfer to on a permanent basis in order to receive Government assistance. Baker Lake was one such centre and Sandy knew it was the beginning of the end of his life in the Arctic.

"I know they need the food. I know it's the only humane thing to do but in the end this welfare will destroy them," he fretted during one of his long discourses with his new assistant, Duncan Pryde, who was, in time, to become an acclaimed author and champion of the Inuit people. "I worry that in a way I've been responsible for this dreadful change. We fur traders encouraged them to trap rather than hunt, to come to the posts to trade for goods they previously had no need for." A pause and then: "But they still depended on the caribou, didn't they?" he mused, more to himself than to the young man who was trying hard to understand the older man's distress. "And the deer just changed their route. You know," he confided, back with Duncan again, "the biologists have studied this phenomenon and they have no explanation for it. It's incredible and it's the tragedy of these people. No longer the people of the deer, soon to become the people of the welfare cheque, aimless, listless..." His voice broke and turned from Duncan. "Better get on into the storeroom, lad. Standing here, bemoaning the fate of a nation isn't going to help anyone, is it?"

Akumulik heard it all and although she did not understand the conversation carried on in English she knew, from the frequent use of the word she did understand – tuktu, caribou – that again Sandy was agonizing over the failure of the caribou. She had her own theory, one she did not voice – too many people to scoff and argue with scientific reasons why it should not be so – but one she was convinced was a regrettable but logical explanation for the disaster. Year after year, from her earliest childhood, she had seen the hunters set off after the caribou, killing without discrimination, killing for the excitement, more deer than they could ever need for food or clothing. Surely, throughout the generations of caribou, a warning had been passed from doe to fawn until finally the herds had learned not to pass through the lands where their ancestors had been butchered. Akumulik firmly believed that the intelligence of the animal had saved it from extinction and that to this day, hundreds of thousands still roamed the remote Barrens, safe from the spears and guns of the People.

Finally it really was time for him to go. There could be no second chances, no "let's give it another few years" return. And the emotion of the moment proved almost too much for him. The entire settlement was at the landing strip when the plane arrived to take him away. A brief hug for Akumulik and then in a loud hoarse voice he declared, "Well, I've spent thirty years of my life here, and I'm glad to be leaving this place. I've got some money saved up. I'm going to take a trip round the world … I never want to see the Arctic again." He sniffed loudly and blew his nose. On the verge of tears, he boarded the plane and turned his head away from the land, the lake and the people that had given him a lifetime of satisfaction and happiness.

Akumulik, aching with unshed tears, walked back to the house, a house that would always be the Red One's, and steeled herself, yet again, for a future without him.

CHAPTER 43

He was not to know, of course, but this was indeed the beginning of the end for Sandy Lunan. He returned to Dunning, to the claustrophobic welcome of his sister Aggie and her daughter Janet, but this time he found he could cope with their rules and petty regulations as he knew it was only temporary. He was planning his trip around the world, an adventure that would keep him away from rural Scotland for about a year. He had also struck up a friendship with David Ogilvie, the husband of his sister Margaret's daughter, who lived about thirty miles away near Dundee. There was a great rapport between the two and Sandy had asked his friend to look out for a reasonable property for him to view on his return. He knew, kind though they were, that he could not live out his life with Aggie and Janet; far better to settle somewhere, on his own, preferably near to David and his wife Rettie. Such an arrangement would prove harmonious for all.

And then he was off. First stop, Canada. He visited relatives; William's wife and two children, now grown into a fine young man and woman; friends on both the east and west coast, ex-colleagues in Winnipeg and Churchill, but he did not return to Baker Lake. It was too soon. The pain he had felt on leaving would stab him with a vengeance and besides he wanted to be more settled, have a definite retirement plan in motion before he went back; stories he could tell the folks at the station, let them know that life did not end just because he had left them and the Arctic. Yes, he would go back, he promised himself, but not just yet. He went on to Australia where brother David now had a large and welcoming family and who was more than happy to show off his brother and let him entertain his

Aupaluktuk - the Red One

friends with weird and wonderful stories of the Arctic wilderness.

It had been a good trip, one which he thought would take the itch out of his feet, certainly for a year or two. But somewhere along the line he picked up an infection. Back with Aggie and Janet he kept his discomfort to himself until it was no longer possible to deceive doctor Janet and, alarmed at his rapid deterioration, she arranged to have him admitted to Perth Royal Infirmary.

But it was too late. A reasonably simple urinary tract infection which, caught early enough, could have been treated with modern antibiotics, raged throughout his body. David and Rettie rushed from Dundee to his bedside. They were just in time. On February 22nd, 1962, he died, aged 67, a little over two years since his retirement.

Janet was inconsolable. She blamed herself. "Why didn't I see it sooner? Why didn't he tell me?" But David, already wise to the nature of his new friend, was pragmatic. "He was a private man, Janet," he consoled. "He couldn't have talked of a thing like that to a slip of a girl, especially his own niece, doctor or no. You've nothing to reproach yourself with, lass. It was just the way he was. And maybe it's all for the best, you know. For all his grand plans he was like a fish out of water here and in no time at all he would have been fretting for a change. He died before his time, that's true, but he certainly made the best of the time he had."

EPILOGUE

We visited Baker Lake in September 1997. It is now a community of well over a thousand people, almost all of them living on welfare. My first impressions were not favourable.

Endless small prefabricated wooden buildings, placed with no apparent order or planning amongst a sea of debris. Rusting fuel barrels, half-gnawed bones, electric cable either surplus to requirements or unearthed due to the permafrost bringing it to the surface. By the lake shore the dilapidated remains of the old Anglican mission now apparently used by the church for Sunday school. Red earth dampened down into roads along which chunter four-wheeled motor bikes open to the elements. Motorised snow sleds, used in the winter, unprotected against rust and weather, temporarily abandoned beside the houses.

The sky and the lake water are leaden grey. A heavy cloud mass hangs over the community and the slight breeze, surprisingly chill, disturbs the dirty sheets of plastic hanging over doorways, sets in motion the tundra grasses, silver, yellow, dull green amongst the tumble of rocks and boulders. A yellow dog tethered to a post stretches and yawns. He seems to spend his sad life permanently attached to the metal post outside his family's house. No one seems to pay him any attention although he rises hopefully, tail wagging, every time he sees any movement around him. Everything looks camouflaged, shades of green and yellow, brown and grey, ochres and terracottas, rusty reds; specks of vivid colour – a large bright blue trampoline outside someone's shack. A building block of children's climbing frames in primary red, blue and yellow, garish and out of place beside the earth tones elsewhere.

And then the sun comes out, the clouds turn to white cotton balls and the lake is transformed to an endless shimmering blue, beautiful, tranquil, beckoning. There is, after all, loveliness here, in the lake, in the smiling open faces of the townspeople, in the bare lichen-covered hillside, uncannily like Scotland. There is a new Northern store opened only this summer filled with produce, beautifully displayed, clean and spacious, run with efficiency and friendliness. There is a spirit, possible only in such a close-knit society, of caring and community. All needs are met – medical, educational, religious. The community hall houses curling and ice hockey rinks, tourists' many demands are catered for with organized boat trips, hunting and camping expeditions, historic trails, arts and crafts centres, comfortable accommodation.

And there is the Akumulik Centre, once the trading post of the Hudson's Bay Company, now a museum telling the story of the life of a fur trader. The store is as it was, offering tins of milk, tea, ammunition, HBC blankets waiting apparently for the first customers of the day. Behind the counter stands Sandy Lunan – a life-size cutout of Baker Lake's most respected and loved post manager.

And so, in essence, he lives on today, frozen in time, in the building bearing the name of his soulmate and companion. A tribute indeed to the Red One.

SOURCES

- Hudson's Bay Company Archives, Manitoba Culture Heritage and Citizenship Provincial Archives - Winnipeg, Canada. Special thanks to Judith H. Beattie - Keeper Hudson's Bay Co Archive.

- National Archives of Canada, Client Services and Communications Branch, Ottowa, Canada.

- Geomatics Canada, Secretarial Geographical Names, Ottowa, Canada.

- I. Rod McDonald, Oakville, Ontario, Canada.

- P. A. C. Nichols, White Stone, VA, U.S.A.

- J. A. Lamb, Rankin Inlet, N.W.T., Canada.

- H. P. Wilson, Edmonton, Alberta, Canada.

- Mrs Isobel McCarter, Victoria, B.C., Canada.

- I. Mouat, Saltspring Island, B.C., Canada.

- E. H. Mitchell, Coldwater, Ontario Canada.

- R. Belcher, Gibsons, B.C., Canada.

- P. W. Nasmyth, Victoria, B.C., Canada.

- Mrs E. Jackson, Peace River, Alberta, Canada.

- B. McMaster, Brighton, Ontario, Canada.

- D. McLauchlin, Calgary, Alberta, Canada.

- Mrs V. Fraser, Frankfort, Ontario, Canada.

- J. M. Gleason, Winnipeg, Canada.

- R. Fotheringham, Bolton, Ontario, Canada.

- R. Hammond Innes CBE, Suffolk, U.K.

- Dr. A. Brand, Antigonish, Nova Scotia, Canada.

- Mike and Betty Hughson, Baker Lake, Northwest Territories, Canada.